NATIONAL GEOGRAPHIC DIRECTIONS

Los Angeles

A . M . HOMES

Los Angeles: People, Places, and the Castle on the Hill

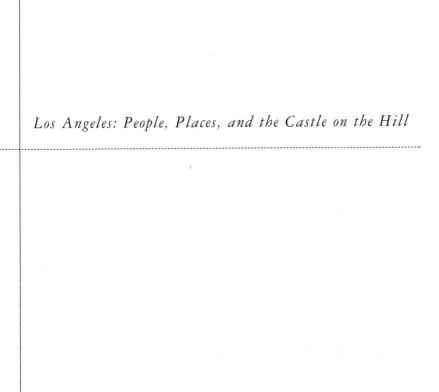

NATIONAL GEOGRAPHIC DIRECTIONS

NATIONAL GEOGRAPHIC
Washington D.C.

Published by the National Geographic Society
1145 17th Street, N.W., Washington, D.C. 20036-4688

Text copyright © 2002 A. M. Homes
Map copyright © 2002 National Geographic Society

Library of Congress Cataloging-in-Publication Data

Homes, A. M.
    Los Angeles : people, places, and the castle on the hill / A.M. Homes
        p. cm. -- (National Geographic directions)
    ISBN 0-7922-6536-X
    1. Los Angeles (Calif.)--Description and travel. 2. Los Angeles (Calif.)--Civilization.
    3. Chateau Marmont (Los Angeles, Calif.) I. Title. II. Series

F869.L84 H66 2002
979.4'94--dc21

                                                                        2002030938

One of the world's largest nonprofit scientific and educational organizations, the National Geographic Society was founded in 1888 "for the increase and diffusion of geographic knowledge." Fulfilling this mission, the Society educates and inspires millions every day through its magazines, books, television programs, videos, maps and atlases, research grants, the National Geographic Bee, teacher workshops, and innovative classroom materials. The Society is supported through membership dues, charitable gifts, and income from the sale of its educational products. This support is vital to National Geographic's mission to increase global understanding and promote conservation of our planet through exploration, research, and education. For more information, please call 1-800-NGS LINE (647-5463), write to the Society at the above address, or visit the Society's Web site at www.nationalgeographic.com.

Interior design by Michael Ian Kaye and Tuan Ching, Ogilvy & Mather, Brand Integration Group

Printed in the U.S.A.

For Marie and Lulu

CONTENTS

Los Angeles

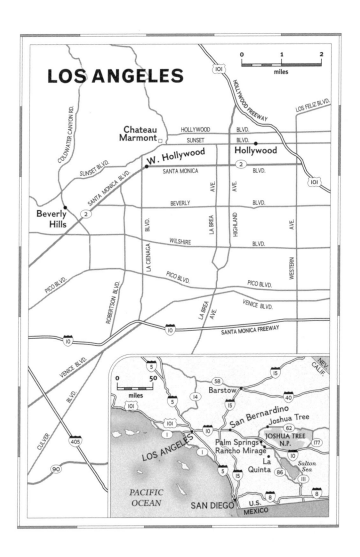

Preface

When National Geographic called and said they'd send me anywhere in the world I wanted to go, the only stipulation being that I write a book about it, I had visions of a walking tour across France, wending my way over hills and through the valleys from château to château. I had fantasies of dogsledding across Canada, the brisk wind biting my face, the heated breath of panting dogs comforting me. I had visions of taking a cruise around the world, stretched out on the deck of a ship the size of a city, conjuring what it is to go full circle, from port to port. When National Geographic called and asked where I wanted to go, I chose Los Angeles.

I chose Los Angeles because it feels like one of the most American cities in America right now. Simultaneously a city of the future and the past, the American Dream continues to thrive here and the city remains a mythological mecca, an epicenter for visionaries, romantics, and dreamers. And Los Angeles is perhaps the most surreal place in America. In fact and fiction, its landscape, hills, and valleys are the backdrop against which our postmodern lifestyle plays itself out and our national anxieties and influences are thrown into relief.

I chose Los Angeles because I had always wanted to live at the Chateau Marmont and dip into my own fantasy life about what it is to call a hotel home. This part for me was an exotic adventure located somewhere between Kay Thompson's Eloise at the Plaza and Vladimir Nabokov living at Le Montreux Palace Hotel in Switzerland. The hotel itself, suspended in time, lost in the glamour of old Hollywood, echoes my questions about the state of the Dream, about how heroes and icons are made and maintained.

Before I even left home, I started to study the city. It quickly became apparent that Los Angeles was a well-traveled, well-studied subject, brilliantly explored by some who have made it their life's work to give order to the disorder, the sprawl. It seemed obvious that as an outsider I could not presume to add to their understanding. My trips became a kind of reconnaissance mission, a visit from the outside. Among my goals was to get to know the city and to explore the notion expressed by Gertrude Stein's comment in *Everybody's Autobiography,* about her hometown of Oakland, California— "there is no there there."

In thinking about how to capture my own Los Angeles, it felt essential to find real "characters" and ask them about their lives. And rather than processing their words and making them my own, I wanted these voices to be represented. The interviews as they appear in the book are edited versions of long-form interviews—"scenes" from my L.A. With every conversation I had, the city of Los Angeles opened, deepened, revealing itself to be far more complicated, peculiar, eccentric, and more human than I'd anticipated.

CHAPTER ONE

Associating with the Positive

The problem with Los Angeles is that it's not in New York. I am a traveler of the mind but not the body.

For ten years I didn't fly. I remained flatfooted, earthbound, as though made of cement, as though flying was the most unnatural thing in the world. The fear came over me suddenly in mid-flight on a trip from Chicago to Washington, D.C. It was night, the plane was on a steady course, the engines droned evenly, and, without warning, I became terrified. I looked out the window into the black velvet night and was convinced the plane was about to crash into a mountain.

As a novelist, in order to write I must first see something in my mind's eye, and in my mind's eye I could see the mountain, I could feel it and I wanted to do something, summon the flight attendant, take evasive action. I glanced around the plane; no one else seemed to be having this thought. Everyone was perfectly calm. I said nothing. The plane continued on and landed safely. But my love affair with travel abruptly ended. Something in me had turned, and for ten years I would not fly. I said no to everything that required getting on a plane— would you like to give a reading in Rome—No. Vacation on a Greek island—No. Spa in Mexico—No. On book tours, I took the train the whole way around the country. I drove enormous distances. I bonded with numerous members of the large and mostly anonymous club of those who would not leave the Earth's surface. But I secretly longed for outer space.

There is a romance to flight, to the image of the aviator as explorer. It is perhaps one of man's strongest impulses to try and free himself from the laws of nature, to defy gravity. We live in a global culture where time and space are compressed, where people commute coast to coast like the Jetsons. It is not unusual for an American to go to London for a single meeting and then turn around and whisk oneself home. Compelled by ambition and desire—we want everything faster and we want it now. And yet it is not entirely natural to climb into an airplane, a souped-up tin can with two hundred and fifty strangers, propel thirty odd thousand feet in the air and push onward at speeds over five hundred miles an hour.

Fear of flying is a distinctly modern condition; the repository for abstract anxieties, a magnet for free radicals of stress, determined to cling to something, to bind. My fear is simple; I am afraid of the plane crashing—more specifically, I am afraid of extreme consciousness, of those final minutes or seconds, knowing this is it. The core fear is primal—a fear of death— but what is one really afraid of when one is afraid of flying? For many people it is claustrophobia, while for others it's a control issue. Flying is not like being in a car or on a train, where you can get out if you don't like the ride. In some ways it's more like being put under general anesthesia; you can't pull yourself out of it, you have to simply give yourself over to the experience and hope for the best.

What's so beguiling about fear is how deeply personal and irrational it is. Impervious to logic or fact, fear refuses reality. People who are afraid of flying are not comforted by the fact that flying is twenty-one times safer than driving. When you're on the plane, holding your breath, thinking—I can't stand this another minute—the fact that millions and millions of people have traveled safely this year alone is not as comforting as it should be.

After ten years of not flying, I didn't feel I'd saved myself from death. Instead I felt as though my world had shrunk, people and places I loved were out of reach. In my mind I went back in time to that flight from Chicago to Washington. For years people had asked me if I'd had a bad flying experience. I'd always said no. Then I had a flash of insight: The bad flying experience had nothing to do with the flight and everything to do with what else was happening in my life at the moment I thought the plane would hit a mountain. But regardless of what I now knew, I remained terrified.

I decided I would fly again—even if it killed me. I would fly business class because of the extra room, I would fly during the day, and I would medicate myself to take the edge off. Someone suggested a series of tapes created by Dr. R. Reid Wilson, a clinical psychologist in North Carolina—*Achieving Comfortable Flight*. My favorite is tape three side one:

"Associating with the Positive." This is a private time, a special time, an opportunity for you to look toward your positive future, to build the kind of support that you desire for your goals in your long and healthy future."

Associate with the positive. Begin by telling yourself to forget the hell of making the reservations—twenty-seven minutes on hold, "speaking or touching" my frequent-flier number, being disconnected and having to start again from scratch. Amelia Earhart surely didn't have to go through this.

At the airport, there are a lot of news trucks outside.

"What happened?" I ask the woman at the ticket counter.

"We had an incident last night."

"What kind of an incident?"

"Someone tried to bring something onto the plane they shouldn't have—a hazardous substance."

"A liquid?" I ask.

"Something gaseous," the woman at the ticket counter says. "It's OK, we've had a change of equipment."

I nod. At the security check I lift my carry-on to the x-ray belt, step through the metal detector, and then stand still while a woman waves a wand over me—is she scanning me or giving me some sort of electromagnetic blessing?

In the lounge, I size up my fellow passengers—there are children clinging to their father's legs, a flight attendant whose mother is on the flight, and two priests. I wonder about the good-luck quotient: Do two priests neutralize the beefy guy with the gold chain?

Ten minutes before check-in, I go to the desk and explain that I am a fearful flier and ask if I might board a few minutes early.

"Oh," the ticket agent says, "I hate to fly. I used to like it but then I got sick and had to go on medication and I gained all this weight and I haven't been on a plane for two years." He draws a breath. "Go ahead. You can board now."

Throughout the plane there is Zen-like music playing, projections of billowing fields of hay on the movie screen.

As the hordes descend, the flight attendant in Coach bellows, "If you can't find a place for it, it goes below," reminding me of Shelly Winters taking charge aboard the sinking ship in *The Poseidon Adventure.* I look into the Coach section; the seats are like infant car seats or straitjackets. Being seated at the back of a plane with a full Coach section is enough to give anyone an anxiety attack.

I buckle up. I play my tape. "This is a private time ..." I watch the animated film of the emergency evacuation procedures: cartoon people taking off cartoon high heels, sliding down the chute like it's a carnival ride. The flight attendant stands at the front of the cabin gesturing toward the emergency exits, demonstrating the oxygen mask.

Takeoff: I feel the pull of the Earth, gravity, resistance. I hold on tight during the climb, the power turn, and when there is a leveling off, a dropping back of the engines, I can't help but think something is wrong—if we're going to have a massive failure, if we're going to suddenly plummet back to Earth, it will happen at this point. But the plane continues the climb, the chimes ring, the FASTEN SEAT BELT sign goes off, and the flight attendant comes over to me.

"Are you the fearful flier?"

I am embarrassed that perhaps I have gone too far, confessing my phobia to everyone from the reservationist to the baggage handler and the boarding agent.

"It was noted in the computer," the flight attendant says.

I shake my head. "No."

Once we're at cruising altitude I am okay. I wouldn't say that I am relaxed, but I'm perfectly fine until we hit a little turbulence.

"What was that?" I ask the flight attendant.

"Light chop, the pilot calls it. Par for the course."

I am looking out the window, up at the wild blue, at the horizon line, at the Earth below. From the galley comes the smell of freshly baked muffins—in business class they bake cookies and muffins, feeding you every two hours as though you were a newborn. I am falling in love with flying all over again. Below us the Earth is otherworldly, a kind of reddish, craggy clay surface, a lunar landscape, shadows and deep crevices.

"Passing over the Grand Canyon," I say to the woman next to me. "It's pretty spectacular from thirty-three thousand feet."

"It's not the Grand Canyon," the woman says, just as the pilot's voice comes over the public address system and announces, "For those of you on the right side of the plane, you'll see that we're passing over the Grand Canyon, quite a sight from thirty-three thousand feet."

I hear the Joni Mitchell song, "Amelia," in my head, the line about how, like me, "she had a dream to fly."

The sun on the wings, the sparkling perfection of the sky, the true majesty of it, unique, ever changing, wholly original and enormous, the beauty, the mystery of it, dwarfs any fears, as does the drone of the engines, which has a kind of white noise, soporific numbing or muting effect. It is like the sound of a vacuum cleaner, a sound which is hard to be tense above or over.

The flight attendant brings the little old lady next to me a kosher meal.

"I'm not Jewish," the woman confides. "A friend taught me to order this—it's always fresher."

I nod.

"Would you like some fruit?" she asks.

And then we are descending, and the city comes into focus, economies as seen from above. There is the geography, the land and the breakdown of the land into lots. It is every man for himself. There are neighborhoods with sharp metal fences; houses close together with small yards filled with discarded stuff, refrigerators, cars, parts of things. There are palatial spreads with high brick walls, country clubs, shopping centers, and swimming pools, lots of swimming pools: above ground, below ground, circular, kidney shaped, long narrow lanes of water.

By the time I arrive in Los Angeles, I'm thrilled. I've done what I didn't think I could ever do again, but it is not enough to do it once, like a trick, a feat of enormous will. I will have to do it again. As the plane is landing I'm thinking, I'd like to continue on. I wonder what it would be like to stay suspended for days, to fly around the world, moving from airport to airport, hearing announcements in a dozen languages, noting the costume changes of the travelers, the shifting menu selections, riding the curve of the Earth's surface.

CHAPTER TWO

Transient Spaces

"Current conditions in Los Angeles, haze with winds east-northeast at eight miles per hour and a ground temperature of fifty-five degrees. We ask that you stay seated until we come to a complete stop at the gate and the pilot has turned off the seat belt sign. When deplaning take care to note that items in the overhead bin may have shifted during flight so please open carefully. For those of you making connecting flights to Palm Springs, Sacramento, and San Francisco, please stop at the desk on your way out for gate information."

I help the old woman next to me get her bag out of the overhead bin.

"Be careful," she says, "it's full. I'm going to visit my sister—she's ninety-three. I'm ninety-one, but I'm in better shape, she's a little hard of hearing and doesn't get around as well. She doesn't drive. I live in New York—no one drives. I bring food. Don't hurt yourself. There's cranberry sauce in my carry-on. I made it last night. We weren't together for Christmas, so I thought I'd make a nice meal."

Crowds gather on the other side of the ropes, dividing ticketed passengers from non-travelers. Looking expectantly toward the gates they remind me of nightclub wanna-bes pressing at the velvet ropes. They have the same kind of optimistic, vulnerable expression, waving their hands as if begging to be chosen—pick me, pick me.

A group of men stands holding plastic placards with people's names written in black grease pen. These are the drivers. If you're having an egomaniacal departure from reality, you might think these are your fans. Many people seem to approach them that way, as though they will be asked to shake hands and sign autographs.

I see my name on one of the placards and nod to the man. We meet at the space where the rope opens.

"Do you have any luggage?" he asks.

Waiting at the baggage carousel, I make the same kind of small talk you'd have with an orderly about to wheel you down the hall for a "procedure"—distracted, distant but friendly, not wanting to be either intrusive or noncommunicative.

"Nice flight?" he asks.

I nod. I notice the little old lady who was next to me looking for her luggage. I begin noticing how people tie things onto their suitcases, ribbons, pieces of yarn, how they sometimes paint a big white dot on the side, identifiers, tribal marks.

"What color are your bags?" the driver asks.

"Black," I say—it is a little like going to a coat check without your number and saying your coat is wool.

I see the woman from the plane struggling to pull her bag off the belt. I grab it for her. It is an old, mustard-colored, vinyl suitcase shaped just right to hold a couple of bowling balls.

"Steady," she says. "There's a frozen turkey in there."

I hand the big bird over and she's on her way.

Two bags come crashing down the luggage chute, competing to land and bounce off the conveyer belt. Weirdly, as soon as I see the bags, I know one is mine.

"That's mine," I say as I see them slam down onto the conveyer belt. I see someone else's hand touch the bag, turn it over, looking. "Mine," I shout, frightening him away.

I wait with my winter coat draped over my arm while the driver goes to get the car. Everything appears to be climate-controlled—the plane, the airport, the atmosphere itself. I am not hot, I am not cold. I am not sweating. In fact, I am barely breathing.

As a New Yorker, as a former child of suburbia, it amazes me that I stand at the curb waiting while a man I don't know goes to get the car and that when he pulls up, I willingly climb in. Does it make sense to let a stranger pick you up in a long black car? And equally, does it make sense that most often, they do take you where you want to go?

I move from one vacuum-sealed environment to another—my feet have not touched earth since I left New York this morning. I'm traveling as though I am an object, a painting, some precious breakable thing, plastic-wrapped, heavily protected, deeply American.

Acceleration: the car peels away from the curb and once again I feel the pull of gravity; I feel some piece of me has been left behind.

The back seat is plush—thick leather seats, a basket of goodies, water, candy, an apple, Wash 'n Dries, all the things you'd find in a good hotel mini-bar.

From the moment you arrive in Los Angeles, it is about the car. From the back seat I call Enterprise and arrange for them to deliver my rental car to the hotel. This is a place where you don't want to be without a means of transportation, you don't want to be without a way out, not even for a moment.

Just as London, Paris, and New York stood as symbols for past centuries, Los Angeles is the city for the twenty-first century. Hovering at the farthest edge of the Wild West, Los Angeles is the home of the American Dream machine— Hollywood—it is where hopes and desires are manufactured and delivered back as though they were our own, where lucky men and women are elevated, as if elected, to become our stars, our heroes—at least until someone better comes along.

For hundreds of years, explorers and pioneers, beginning with Franciscan monk Junípero Serra, on through Jedediah Smith, the ill-fated members of the Donner party, missionaries, gold rushers, early motion-picture makers, dust-bowl immigrants, aircraft engineers, entrepreneurs, adventurers, rebels and radicals, gurus and groupies, have all come to California in search of something. They come looking for something other, something more. They come rushing from what is to what might be, each one carrying their own vision of a utopian idyll. They come to lose themselves, to find themselves; they come in pursuit of fame and fortune. Los Angeles, California—the state itself named after a fictional island of great wealth—is perhaps the closest thing America has to a Promised Land.

The new century began with enormous expectations, almost a sense of entitlement, for continued success, growth, the upsizing of the American Dream. But beneath all of this lurks the threat that the dream has become inflated as if to compensate for all that is otherwise not happening, as if to distract us from an underlying depression—emotional and economic; as though we are consuming, stuffing, and spoiling ourselves to avoid our fear of failing, of falling, of having nothing at all.

Los Angeles exists in this disconnect, in this fissure, like a geological fault in the collective soul. In Los Angeles there is always an inescapable tension just beneath the surface, the sense that something, no one knows exactly what, is about to happen, that it could go one way or the other, that at any moment you could win big or lose it all, that the very foundation of the city, that the bottom could come out from under, that the good life, as good as it gets, could be gone in a minute.

Life in Los Angeles is steeped in twelve-step culture—everything is just for today. You are obliged to take one day at a time; absolutely no one wants to commit to more—not the illegal immigrant housekeeper who knows that at any moment she could be busted and sent back across the border, not the movie executive whose sixty-million-dollar romantic comedy turns out to be a sixty-million-dollar disaster. It is a town that specializes in the suspension of disbelief, the suspension of time, reality, history, memory.

Everyone is a new arrival and there is no welcome wagon—why help the competition? Even the architecture is transient, like stage sets; things can be built in a day and destroyed just as easily. This constant state of flux is in part the result of a radical/rebel willingness to experiment, to tolerate all styles and sensibilities at once—after all, California is in many ways the American outback.

It is a place of enormous anonymity—people pass each other blindly on their way in and out of their homes, on and off the freeways. And yet people are desperate for recognition. They want to be seen, noticed—they are constantly hawking their product, pitching their services, their souls. They want to be recognized, rewarded, congratulated. One can't help but wonder if the notoriously profound narcissism of Angelenos is exacerbated by the disconnect.

"The story you're about to see is true. Only the names have been changed to protect the innocent." This is the city where Jack Webb played Sergeant Joe Friday, a cop working the late shift on *Dragnet*; where Jack Klugman played Quincy, Deputy Chief L.A. Medical Examiner; where Charlie's Angels played the sexiest of private eyes; where the attorneys on *L.A. Law* work overtime to settle the score.

This is a city with an infamous dark side, shadowy figures, hard-boiled noir, the Black Dahlia, the helter-skelter of the Manson family killings. This is the city where fact turns to fiction, twists and turns, and then fiction turns to fact. This is where "Reality TV" was born. This is where O. J. Simpson's car chase was broadcast live from a helicopter tracking the Ford Bronco as it made its way over the city's infamous freeways.

And it is the place where a former President "removed from public view" is holed up in a Bel Air mansion, evaporating, slowly pulling back from reality as we know it.

It is simultaneously a city of the future and a city of the past, with all the attendant complications—racial, economic, social, and cultural—of any major American city. And yet at a time when other cities are shrinking back, Los Angeles is coming into its own, expanding, thriving.

I am drawn to Los Angeles as though it were a character I am compelled to crawl inside of, exploring its evolution, the people who populate it, the land itself, as though to inhabit it, however briefly, will allow me to make sense of it. I am drawn to it for all the wrong reasons, just like those who have visited before me, intrigued, horrified by the glitter, the shine, the strangeness.

The first time I came to Los Angeles, I hated it. It was Christmas vacation—I was still in school. I flew west to visit my best friend from childhood. I remember being stunned by the cold, the damp, the rawness of the city without winter. No one talks about it, but instead of winter, L.A. has what can only be described as a rainy season, which arrives sometime in January and leaves by the middle of February. By the end of it, everything starts to smell.

I also remember the houses built into the sides of hills, looking at them half in awe, half horrified, not knowing if their placement was terrifically stupid, smart, naïve, or boldly optimistic. In a place where the land is so unstable, it seems incredibly presumptuous to pin houses to the sides of hills, as though they will not slip, will not lose their footing, will not slide onto the house just below—many seemed to be hanging by a thread.

On that first trip, we did the classic California tourist things: Disneyland, whale-watching, the San Diego Zoo, shopping at stores owned by celebrities—as though they'd be there behind the counters saying, "And what can I do for you today?" We touched the ground at various famous intersections, as if that was history in the making. We strolled the Hollywood Walk of Fame, checking to see whose star was next to whose. At Mann's Chinese Theatre, formerly Grauman's Chinese Theatre, the stars signed their names and set their feet in cement—Hedy Lamarr, Judy Garland—leaving their footprints like markers, proof. Outside the theater there were souvenir stands, merchants from all over the world hawking memorabilia as though it was a food stuff, an essential like chicken or rice. Everything was about buying the memories, mementos to bring back home, to prove that you were there. Much less glamorous than you'd imagine it to be, all of it was seedier and more downtrodden than depicted in the issues of *Rona Barrett's Hollywood* and *Tiger Beat* that I'd grown up poring over. Old Hollywood—drunks, derelicts, depressing.

We went on the Universal Studios tour, and sat on a tram that wound in a circle around the lot, clearly not really the lot, but a heavily narrated theme park. "On your left, the lake where Jaws lives, on your right ye old Bates Motel and just up the hill, the Gothic house from *Psycho*. Notice the Old West, our Mexico, and your small hometown street." All of it deserted, showing no signs of ever having been used, the facade of a back lot. Entirely separated from the actual moviemaking process, there wasn't a chance of seeing a star arriving for work, of being spotted, plucked out of the crowd and invited for lunch at the commissary. I posed in a machine that put my picture on the cover of *Time* magazine as Woman of the Year. I also posed for *People* and *Us*. I posed wondering—am I pretending this is real? Am I going to bring these images home? Would anyone believe me—Oh, yes, I was gone for a week and became a national hero? There is something distinctly American about our need to put our faces on everything from faux celebrity portraits to currency, T-shirts, etc. It is all about the fantasy of being famous, of being "somebody."

At Christmas, some people in Los Angeles paint their lawns white, like snow. In the winter, the rich go to the mountains where there is snow, to their outposts in Aspen, Sundance, and Switzerland, and the rest make do, spraying fake snowflakes on their windows, hanging wreaths on their doors.

On that first visit, I went to a Christmas Eve midnight mass at an Episcopal church on Sunset Boulevard. On the way there, I mistook the boy hookers for hitchhikers and suggested that we give them a ride. The priest leading the service walked up the aisle swinging the incense hypnotically back and forth, as though he was luring me in. I remember looking at the people around me, an odd amalgam of humanity, gathered on a dank and drizzly midnight to celebrate the birth of Jesus. They were dipping up and down, threadbare knees pressing against the kneeler, singing and swaying along. I remember looking around, breathing deeply and chanting to myself—this is not for me, this is not for me.

I come out of my fugue, of the past—where are we?

All I see is a low flat expanse, a colorless sky and miles of asphalt unfolding. There is a lack of landscape, lack of an organizing idea, a focus. This absence of a center furthers the often referenced notion that there is no "there" here. Natives would argue, rightfully, that there is a "there" everywhere. Los Angeles is a city of a thousand cities, but until you know that, until you know how and where one enters, the surface all looks the same, one building after another, one mini-mall, one car wash. It all begins to look familiar, the repetition becomes a rhythm, pulling me closer. We pass the Flynt Publications building, a modern oval structure, home to *Hustler* magazine. I think of the movie *The People vs. Larry Flint,* where Larry Flynt was shot, paralyzed by a sniper's bullet. Was it in front of this building or on the steps of a Georgia courthouse? In the movie, actor Woody Harrelson plays Flynt; he does a good job. I can no longer remember the true story, can no longer sort fact from fiction; I take that as a mark of the film's success.

"Business or pleasure," the driver says when he sees I'm looking around.

"A little of both," I say. "What's news," I ask, catching his eye in the rearview mirror—have I had this driver before?

"Academy Awards are coming soon," he says. "Everyone is getting ready. It's a bigger deal than Christmas. They're already shopping, the hotels are booked, we bring in extra cars from Las Vegas to meet the demand."

"What else are you working on?" Whether or not I have had this driver before, a driver is always more than a driver. Everyone in Los Angeles is not what they first appear to be.

"Writing a script with an actor friend," he says. "And I've got a feature that I'm producing. We start shooting in three weeks. I have the shooting script in the trunk—I'll give you one. We got a great response. Julia Roberts may even give us a cameo. I drove her once."

Really, that's all it takes? A ride from the airport and you're signed?

The long black car makes a left off Sunset Boulevard onto Marmont Lane and slips into the small driveway of the Chateau Marmont—practiced, he has made this run before.

My door is opened, the trunk is popped, and I hope no one besides me is disappointed that my steamer trunks, my load of Louis Vuitton, turn out to be two Travel Pro suitcases on wheels—borrowed from a friend.

"How are you?" the bellhop asks. I have been here before— multiple times. The garage is the portal to the hotel; everyone passes through it.

"I had to fly," I say. There is a part of me that thinks I should get extra credit for flying; the hotel should be so glad I arrived safely that they put me in the penthouse. "We thought you'd be more comfortable here," the bellman might say.

"Welcome back," he says. "Do you want to check in and I'll bring these to your room?"

The Castle on the Hill—its tarnished patina is a kind of cultural comment. It ages more than gracefully, its earthquake-proof walls absorbing the stuff of scandal, turning its tainted past into a luscious history.

Among my earliest images of the Chateau Marmont is March 5, 1982. John Belushi in a body bag. His enormous dead weight apparent as a white-sheeted gurney is rolled down Marmont Lane to a van from the Los Angeles Coroners office. The finality of the black bag, zipped, the circumstances of his death a defining mark, the end of an era.

The Chateau Marmont was the place where rock stars didn't sleep, staying up for hours, partying after the show, trashing the already trashy rooms. Led Zeppelin reportedly rode their motorcycles through the lobby; Jim Morrison jumped off a bungalow roof and into the pool—or off a terrace onto the ground, depending on who tells the story. In either version he was so high that he didn't hurt himself—he just bounced. This was where James Dean first read the script for Nicholas Ray's *Rebel Without a Cause* with Natalie Wood. Instinctively, I always knew this is where I would stay. This was the place you went to lose your mind, to become yourself. The Chateau Marmont is still the spot where they all come, a tourist attraction, a rite of passage, a home away from home.

Checking into the hotel is like stepping into a living history. It is out of time, suspended from the constraints, the issues, the concerns of the real world. One immediately calms down here. The relaxation response is a phenomenon reported by numerous guests—as soon as they arrive, they feel better. It's hard to know why that is—the laid-back, low-key staff, the noirish interiors, crushed velvet sofas that seem to seep stories—you can picture the girl and her gangster boyfriend, the rock star and his groupie, the junkie, the reclusive millionaire. Anything and everything can and does happen here.

"I mean, it was built for, you know, peccadilloes," says writer Eve Babitz, a longtime friend of the hotel. "So obviously the people who built it knew what they were doing. You know, if you want to commit suicide, if you want to commit adultery, go to the Chateau. It was the height of elegance. Elegant and swellegant. It's international. And it's not afraid. It doesn't mind brilliant talent, or romance, or lunacy."

From its very beginnings the Chateau Marmont was a peculiar sort of folly. Commissioned by Fred Horowitz and designed by architect Arnold A. Weitzman, it was modeled after Château d'Amboise in France's Loire Valley. An old and infamous royal residence, Château d'Amboise is believed to be the final resting place of Leonardo da Vinci. The Chateau Marmont, slightly more modest, was built in the late 1920s as Los Angeles's first earthquake-proof apartment building and was converted to a hotel in the 1930s. The hotel's reputation as the place to go to misbehave dates back to the days of the Motion Picture Code of the 1930s and the purity seal of 1934. The code specified not only what could and could not be shown on screen, but also its expectations of a star's behavior off camera. Studios rented apartments and rooms for the express purpose of having someplace safe for their stars to engage in whatever nasty little habits they had. The famous example being Harry Cohn, head of Columbia Pictures, telling two of his randiest young stars, William Holden and Glenn Ford, "If you must get into trouble, do it at the Chateau Marmont."

When it wants to, Hollywood can be exceptionally good at keeping its own secrets. The Chateau, with its own eccentric and highly personal history, was the perfect coconspirator. With its external appearance of a castle or Gothic fort, combined with its residential past, incredibly thick walls, discreet entry, and highly protective staff who treated guests like members of the family, the Chateau Marmont became the ideal hideout. European guests found the architecture familiar and comforting, sexual outsiders felt accepted, the exceptionally shy were shielded, and anyone else with a reason to hide simply blended into the woodwork—from the start there was the feeling of a shared sensibility. Greta Garbo felt comfortable here, as did Howard Hughes.

This peculiar charm was passed on over the years through a small group of interesting, if eccentric, owners. The service and room conditions ranged from high style to deep dilapidation before landing in the able hands of New York hotelier Andre Balazs in 1991. Balazs put the hotel through a major renovation, seeking to both modernize and preserve the history, and in the end successfully returned the hotel to its original glamour. A mark of that success is that when you ask hard-core fans of the hotel what's different about it now from the 1970s, they say nothing. And while it is true that much of the hotel staff has been here for years—testament to the feeling of family and their dedication—everything in fact is different, the carpets, the furniture, the lighting fixtures, telephones, etc.

"Ha! Well, I've been staying there for … thirty years," says filmmaker John Waters. "And I'm mad they charge you to park your car overnight. That's my only quote. No, just kidding. That's my pet peeve about it. But it is really the place where everyone stays that hates L.A., if you're from Europe, from New York. And all the people that love L.A. don't understand why you ever want to stay there. They think it's

horrible when they come there, they're snobs about it. The whole point is that the Chateau Marmont is reverse snobbery against L.A."

Among the guests, there are always people from New York. Familiar faces, people you've met at parties, come up to you in the lobby, "You're a friend of Sofia's, of John's, of Rob's. Didn't I meet you at Wendy's, with my friend Julie? What are you doing out here?"

There are far fancier hotels in this city of transients, but this place is home. In fact, it's better than home—it's home away from home, and with it comes the fantasy of having, at least temporarily, left your cares behind. I like this hotel for many of the same reasons that originally drew me to New York from my hometown of Washington, D.C. Washington is a self-conscious city, uptight, deeply khaki, essentially afraid of its own shadow, a company town much in the same way that Los Angeles is or believes itself to be. In L.A. there's a myopic tendency to think that the movie business is the only business, forgetting, of course, farming, aerospace, the arts, and anything and everything else. Long ago, when I thought about where I would live when I grew up, I knew it would be New York—a big city, expansive, wild. In New York, I would never be the one on the farthest edge; whatever I did with my life would seem middle of the road, but in Washington, I was among those on the periphery, the fringe. In Los Angeles, it is the same, I am that dark and mystical thing, a woman from the East, an "intellectual."

And yet at the Chateau Marmont, they've seen it all and then some. The hotel is like an apartment building, a halfway house for creative people who can't live alone, and I am the faux little old lady, the librarian living upstairs—there is deep comfort in being the blue-haired woman among the wild ones.

"I've put you on the seventh floor," the man at the front desk says.

"Is there anything else open?" I automatically ask. I have the need to see every available room. At the Chateau, what you get is the luck of the draw. You can't reserve a specific room in advance, and since every room is so different, it's worth checking to see what else is open. They never really know when someone is going to check out—guests at the Chateau have a way of lingering for days, weeks, months, years.

"When I was growing up in Los Angeles, the hotel was always sort of a part of our lives," says filmmaker and actor Griffin Dunne. "You know how some families have these uncles, they're not really their uncles, but you say uncle. Our uncle was a guy named Uncle Earl, who was Earl McGrath. And Earl and Camilla lived on the fifth-floor penthouse. I was there recently and I was told it was the largest terrace space in Los Angeles. It looks exactly the same now as it did then. I mean, they might have gotten a new rug, but they got the same crappy new rug. And the same kind of secondhand-feeling furniture. But that's where they lived. It was very kind of exotic to us that there were people who lived year round in a hotel. It felt kind of a bit of an adventure, every time we went there. If you're a kid it's like going to a castle. Earl and Camilla's place was very much like being in the turret of a castle. Also, the Strip at that time was happening, there was so much to see. I've always been such a die-hard fan of rock and roll and I knew that the Doors stayed there, and Janis Joplin. All these older people were my gods. I remember hearing stories about Jim Morrison

jumping out the fourth-floor window and not breaking a leg—these were things that made it feel legendary."

There is about hotels the sense of a second chance, an opportunity for re-invention; you check in as someone else, an alias, another character, if only for a night. Suspended from yourself, from your everyday life, you have the chance to be a king or queen, to be waited upon hand and foot, unless of course you check into a Motel 6, Best Western kind of thing where there's a noisy ice machine at the end of the hall and a big neon sign that says FREE TELEVISION AND AIR CONDITIONED.

As a kid, I was always fascinated by the peculiarities of hotels' sani-wrapped drinking glasses—for your comfort and pleasure—the toilets with a paper strip across the bowl to prove they've been cleaned, the thin veneer of wood paneling, meant to give the feel of a rustic mountain cabin. Hotel, motel, motor lodge, where you park just outside your room, the motel court with the rooms in a wide half circle, like a wagon train stopped for the night, pulling close for security.

The best hotels have exaggerated amenities: heated towel racks, bottles of water by the side of the bed, treats on your pillow, fresh fruit in the room, stationery with your name printed on it—a list of things you might like doing while you're there, a treat they remembered you especially liked the last time around, new little gifts every day. ...

But whether it is the highest end or a highway special, one always feels a ghostly sense that someone has been there before you, that these rooms belong to no one. The absence of ownership, of care, is perhaps why people feel free to trash them, to steal from them, to behave so differently in them than the way they would at home. There are hotels for the tawdry affair, hotels for sweet sixteens, hotels for wedding nights. And then there are hotels like the Chateau Marmont, where you lie down to sleep and conjure those who lay there before you, you perform as you might imagine they performed, you feel visited in the night by the ghosts of guests past.

"You feel the haunted quality," says photographer Todd Eberle, a frequent guest at the hotel. "There are a lot of ghost stories. You feel like you're sleeping with everyone who ever slept there."

The bellman carries the master key. He lets me into my room—every room has a thousand stories. I remind him that later I want to see all the empty rooms.

The door to the room next door is open. It is in the process of being cleaned. I glance in. The bed has not yet been stripped. It's rumpled, thoroughly slept in. There is a pile of newspaper on the floor, some towels. It has the feel of a crime scene, stumbled upon after the fact—you can't help but wonder, what happened here? Who did what to whom? Stories ooze out of the carpet, out of the walls.

The maid hauls a big bag of trash into the hall.

What is the biggest mess they've ever seen, the oddest sight they've come upon? Are they trained to act as though nothing's happened? What is the largest thing someone's stolen? How do they count the sheets, the towels? What do people do with all the towels that they bring home? Does anyone know someone who's been billed for a towel?

I am a hotel person, a kind of a hotel fetishist. I use them for escape, for meditation, as a place to run away, to hide, to contemplate big decisions. It started when I was a teenager—during a particularly difficult time, I left my parents' house and checked into a nearby Holiday Inn. I spent the evening smoking pot, eating ice cream, and wondering what to do with my life. Later, when I was slightly older, I borrowed my parents' car and took off for the Delaware shore in the dead of winter, checked into a fancy high-rise hotel, and pretended I was a rock star, ordering tequila sunrises from room service, walking on the boardwalk in the blustery wind, and again thinking about what I would do with my life.

There is something about stepping out of your ordinary life and into the suspension of hotel life that allows you distance, perspective, a chance to look in on yourself, to act with a certain remove.

In the early days, I used hotels to act out my cowboy fantasies, and now in my advancing age, I've settled for being treated like royalty. I've developed aesthetic allergies. If a hotel doesn't feel right, if the rooms are overwhelmingly generic, if they depress the hell out of me, I have to get out of there right away. My reaction is immediate and severe, a brand of artful anaphylaxis. In general, I am such a creature of habit, a person so profoundly affected by my surroundings that I cannot bear the discomfort, the disassociation, the anxious fracture that comes from feeling uncomfortable about where I am. It is strange enough to be miles from home. I want a hotel room to comfort me, to make a strange city familiar, to make everything all right at the end of a long day. I want it to hold me very well.

I have arrived in distant cities in the middle of the night and checked in and out of hotels within an hour. I've been led to my room, only to use it for ten minutes to get on the phone, get out my book with lists of hotels and call around town. I've taken tours of every empty room, have moved from hotel to hotel in the wee hours of the morning. I have driven friends crazy with it—Why can't it wait until morning? It's as though there will be no morning unless this is solved immediately. There are hotels that could kill you with their lack of affect, their absence of personality.

I once arrived in San Francisco near midnight. I was both on book tour and on deadline for a magazine article. I had phoned ahead and said I would need a room with a desk in it—the bellman pointed to a tiny table framed with a lighted make-up mirror. "Your desk." As I peered into the mirror, the room began to howl, to literally whine.

"Wind," the bellman said. "She blows in the wind."

I unzipped my suitcase, took out the volume listing all the good hotels in America, and started dialing.

In Edinburgh, I stayed at a hotel that came highly recommended, but when I lay down to sleep, I felt a kind of crawling that caused first my arms, then legs to jerk reflexively. After fifteen minutes of doing a certain spasmodic dance I realized that it was the sheets, the bed, crawling with no-see-ums. I wrapped myself in my raincoat, spread my suit jacket under my head and called it a night.

In Paris, a friend raved about a particular hotel—a room at the top with a terrace. For months I faxed back and forth trying to secure the room. At first it was not available and then at the last minute it was. I envisioned opening the windows out onto a classic Paris street—bellowing, "Who Will Buy?" from *Oliver!* I arrived, the elevator was big enough for one person and one suitcase; it let us off at the floor below ours, we wound our way up a spiral staircase. And the room—the room was dark, dank, and everything in it was a leftover from a garage sale. The terrace was tiny, really more of a big windowsill than anything else. I sat on the bed, made a huge sighing sound, and sank.

In the room next door a baby began to scream, to howl. I could feel the mold spores from the carpet rising up into my nose, lodging in my lungs. And once again I took out the guidebook. I dialed fast and furious. At this point, if I was going to give up this great deal, if I was going to go through the trouble of changing, I wanted something really nice. I called every major hotel and asked what they had available. We left our bags and went on a tour of every room in the city before deciding on the Montalambert. We took a suite, the windows opened up onto a beautiful view, there were birds singing, the sounds of church bells. It was truly fantastic—and of course cost four times more than the first hotel.

The phone rings, pulling me out of my reverie.

It's Benedict, at the front desk. "Your car is here. The rental agent is waiting for you in the lobby."

"What color is it?" I told the rental agency I'd take anything but white.

"White."

"I'll be right down."

CHAPTER THREE

Please Remain Calm

In the elevator at the Chateau Marmont there is a sign—IN CASE
OF EARTHQUAKE PLEASE REMAIN CALM.

The elevator itself is small, a single car accommodating
two to six people, or fewer people and more luggage. The walls
are a deep maroon and trimmed with ornate tin, like decorative
strips of ribbon. On the back wall are picture frames that hold
that day's covers of *Variety* and *Billboard*—the headlines written
in the code of the biz—Head Honcho Axed. Indie Surprise.
Julia Inks Big Deal.

Please Remain Calm. I immediately jot it down in my
notebook.

The idea of an earthquake has been bothering me since before I left New York. Stepping out of the car and onto the ground
in Los Angeles, I felt tentative. That first footstep was a test—
my foot touching the surface, testing to make sure it is solid,

not quick to give way, not already rumbling. In my suitcase, I have a pile of printouts, a seismic hazards map showing probable earthquakes from 1994 to 2024. I am looking at them, trying to read them, like a layman trying to interpret an EKG—heart waves from the center of the Earth. I've been reading information on strong motion, the Earth's crust—what affects the shaking is the softness of the ground, the thickness of sediments below.

Strange things happen here, large events on a kind of biblical scale, and the size and sprawl of the city seems not only to accommodate it, but rather to absorb it.

"It's very *Ten Commandments*," one of my friends says.

"When I was staying there doing this show, 2000 Malibu Road and Joel Schumacher was directing, he said he was thinking about the Bible and the devil," Jennifer Beals tells me, from a cell phone on location in Canada. "As a kid I had read the Bible a lot, and I said you know, there are not that many references to the devil. And we started to go over it, and I said, when I get home tonight I'm going to take out the Bible in the room, look at it, and see what I can find. And that night I went back to this room, I opened the Bible, and at the front of the Bible, on the Chateau Marmont stationery, it says 'I hope you enjoy reading this as much as I do,' and it was signed Hunter S. Thompson. So I went through the Bible ... and I was reading about the devil and reading about the devil and reading about the devil, and I got really tired. And it was one of those things where I fell asleep with all my clothes on in bed with the Bible next to me. And in my dream I feel the room shaking, and I'm scared to open my eyes, because I know that the devil will be at the end of my bed. And I get really brave and I open my eyes, and I realize it's just an earthquake."

It's something about the weather. What was once the stuff of the farmer's almanac is now a television channel all its own, a subject that requires constant monitoring, anxiety, and anticipation. The chance of rain, the allergy index, the brush fire equation, the rise and fall of the tides, El Niño/La Niña, brush fires, mud slides, apocalyptic disaster, indexes for humidity, for wind chill. Add to the weirdness that these phenomena bring the notion that people choose to live in Los Angeles because of the weather. The weather is one of the city's selling points, one of the prime quality-of-life advertisements for living here. The weather is described as perfect, consistently sunny and bright. Furthering the mixed message is the psychological fact that a lot of people who live in L.A. are obsessed with repetition, dependability, the sameness of their routines. They are creatures of habit who can't bear it when things are out of their control, when they have to adjust. When you stop to look carefully, a lot of people in Los Angeles are prone to temper tantrums when they don't get their way. Despite their age and or seeming success, they behave like children. A certain tolerance for this behavior appears one to be one of the underlying organizational factors, one of the personality principles of the city. It occurs to me that these folks might look at weather phenomena as the temper tantrums of the gods, as something they relate to on a primal level (given that they aspire to one day become one of the gods), and so when weather happens, it in fact impresses them, stuns them, and then calms them. The potential scale of a disaster is one of the few things that makes an impression—Los Angeles is very much about size and comparison.

And yet there exists this constant threat. They live with it, building houses on the sides of cliffs, navigating as though challenging the possibility, tempting it on some level, convinced it won't happen to them.

"My other favorite memory," John Waters tells me as we're talking about the Chateau Marmont, "is that I was there in an earthquake and I heard somebody just upstairs go 'yahoo!' Which was such a Chateau moment that it was like they were on an amusement park ride. Not a national disaster ..."

What is the fear of an earthquake? Is it that the Earth will open and you'll fall into a bottomless crevasse, to the center of the Earth? Is it that you'll be on a highway, on an overpass, and it will crumble beneath you and leave you hanging from an edge? Is it the sound of it, the rumble, a rolling thunder like a heart beating too fast? Is it things falling, objects taking flight, the temporary suspension of gravitational laws—that a building will collapse, that something will hit you on the head? Is it the shaking, the non-amusement of having to ride the up and down, the side to side, the bucking/buckling beneath your feet? Is it being cut off, the telephone going dead, the bulb in the refrigerator going black? Is it that no one will be able to reach you, to rescue you? Is it the potential for chaos, explosions, gas fires, water main breaks, looting, man-made eruptions, events that make a rolling blackout look like a cocktail party prank? Is the biggest fear that California itself will break away and become an island floating off the coast of America and you will be left on this geographic raft (fantasy land), this sinking ship with no way back to shore (reality)? Is it that all of this will happen without warning, you could be in the bathroom, on the Stairmaster, in the grocery store, in the middle of a meeting, having a facial, giving birth to a baby?

How long since the last one? Are we overdue? There is always the inevitability of it—an earthquake will happen, it is just a question of where and when.

How do the people live with the constant threat?

"I've always wished I was at the Chateau when the earthquake happened," Griffin Dunne says. "The last one, ninety-whatever it was. Four or five. I was staying at the Four Seasons. It was about four in the morning ... we all gathered in the lobby and I remember thinking, I'm in the wrong hotel. I wish I was in the Chateau. That lobby would be pretty interesting. You know, people are confronting their own mortality."

I study up on the subject of earthquake preparedness. Practice earthquake drills; get under a sturdy table or desk and grab onto it. Teach yourself to duck, cover, and hold. Make a game of it, called "earthquake," like playing hide-and-seek, to find safe places. Explain to children that an earthquake is a natural event and not anyone's fault. Encourage children to express feelings of fear. Include kids in clean-up activities. Make your evacuation plan, make a list of items you'll carry out. Make a first-aid kit—bandages, antibiotic ointments, things to clean wounds, eye drops, aspirin, gloves, candles, knife, garden hose, portable radio, water, toilet tissue, cash. And another one for the car: fire extinguisher, rope, signal device, whistle, water, snacks.

Protect your property—make sure your foundations are reinforced, tabletop objects are secured. TVs, stereos, chinaware can be held with buckles and safety straps. I picture a family eating breakfast with the plates Velcroed to the table, as though they're on the space shuttle, zero gravity. I imagine everything in a china cabinet glued in place. Beware of toppling bookcases; anchor your furniture to a stud—Brad Pitt and your armoire? Do not use an elevator. In a crowded public place, do not rush for doorways. Stay away from windows (stay away from everything). If you are on a highway, pull over. If you are in a wheelchair, try to get under a doorway, lock the wheels, remove items not securely attached to the chair and cover your head. If you are bedridden, cover up with blankets and pillows—essentially play dead. After the quake try to help others if you can.

Symptoms of anxiety may not appear for weeks or months after a quake and can affect people of any age. Symptoms can include disorientation, confusion, loss of sex drive, gastrointestinal distress, irritability, fatigue, and decreased pleasure in life activities.

Online I find that you can actually go on a tour of earthquake-riddled California, working your way from Cajon Pass in San Bernardino up to Pinnacles National Monument and Hollister in San Benito, and onto Crystal Springs Reservoir up in San Mateo, down through the Devil's Punchbowl in Los Angeles, and San Juan Capistrano in Orange County, to the Salton Sea in Imperial.

Confession: I wouldn't mind a small one, a little rattle, rumble, rock and roll; try it out the way you try out a scary ride, a new sport. I think of it as land surfing.

I need professional help. I call the earthquake man, Thomas Henyey, professor of Geological Sciences and director of the Southern California Earthquake Center. Explaining that I am working on a book on Los Angeles, wanting a better understanding of the land and the people and I'm curious to know more, I ask if I might come see him. "I don't know what your schedule is like," he says, "but I'm free this afternoon. You could come right over and we could talk about things."

"I'll be right there."

On my way out, I'm alone in the elevator with a movie star. I don't realize who he is until ten minutes later and then remember that when we made eye contact he looked disappointed—upset that he hadn't been recognized.

In the garage waiting for my car, I ask a woman if she has an earthquake kit.

"Of course I do."

"What's in it?"

"Two hundred single dollar bills, a roll of quarters, four bars of chocolate, make-up in case I have to sleep in a shelter, toothpaste, and a couple of joints—there's no way I can get through an earthquake without being stoned."

The garage guy pulls up in my white Ford Focus. I feel like I'm working as some sort of undercover government agent. There is no car more generic, less distinctive. Later in the afternoon, I have to trade it in because the radio doesn't work—in fact, almost nothing works. It's entirely plastic and so cheaply made that it doesn't have a light over your head when you open the door. It's a car designed to be driven only to and from an airport rent-a-car counter.

I follow my instructions and head toward USC. It's disconcerting how all the street names sound familiar, Figueroa, Wilshire, Beverly. I know them all from television, from *Dragnet* and *Adam-12*.

Tom Henyey's office is in Science Hall. A cross between an academician and a hard-core scientist, Henyey is rugged and outgoing—the kind of person who spends his time off hiking through wilderness. His walls are covered with maps; there's a large computer monitor, a telephone with numerous lines, and paper everywhere. The report I'd been trying to read, on seismic hazards in southern California, was written by the folks in this office.

> **MR. HENYEY:** Okay, well, let me start from the beginning. First of all, I'm a geophysicist. Historically, my research interests have been on the active geological processes that are going on in southern California. Southern California's just a good natural laboratory.
>
> **MS. HOMES:** Who were the first people who really studied earthquakes?
>
> **MR. HENYEY:** The first really serious study of earthquakes in California began at U.C. Berkeley and at Cal Tech, at about the same time, in the 1930s. There was a very famous scientist at Berkeley by the name of Byerly. And his counterpart here at Cal Tech in the south was a fellow by the name of Beno Gutenberg. And the two of them pretty much started earthquake

studies, Byerly in the north and Gutenberg in the south. We speak today of a Gutenberg-Byerly line, it's kind of like the Mason-Dixon Line. They put in some seismographs and began looking at earthquakes. And before that, of course, was the 1906 San Francisco earthquake. I guess you could argue that really, that was the starting point for earthquake studies.

MS. HOMES: When you want to study an earthquake, or when you want to forecast an earthquake, what do you do? And every time there is an earthquake, I'm sure people come to you and say, well, when's the next one?

MR. HENYEY: Earthquakes are our experiments. We can't, unfortunately go into the laboratory and start an experiment. We have to wait for the earthquakes to come along. So of course we're very excited when an earthquake happens. That's when we acquire data on several things. Exactly what the rupture looked like— if it ruptures the ground's surface, we can actually observe it and detail it and so forth. We look at after-shocks because they tend to form a cloud around the rupture and they give us additional information about the earthquake rupture process itself. Then we like to study the waves as they propagate across the region, because it's the waves that create the ground motions. And in an area like southern California, where the geology's very complex, both at the surface and the subsurface, these waves do all sorts of crazy things.

MS. HOMES: And how does that help you forecast what will happen?

MR. HENYEY: To a large extent, that helps with understanding the ground motions, but it doesn't tell us when and where earthquakes will actually occur. So we have to study the faults too. We have to study the general geological framework, how the plates are moving about, and how the faults are moving over time. And so we have, for example, geologists who go out into the field and actually exhume faults.

MS. HOMES: How deep would you dig?

MR. HENYEY: Most of the major earthquakes break the surface. And when they break the surface they disrupt the near-surface materials. So you can go back, you can find those fault traces. We can cut trenches across them. If we had an earthquake that occurred ten thousand years ago, there's a lot of soil that's developed between now and then. We'll see various different soil horizons that have developed over a multi-thousand year timeframe. And the way we date these things is by and large through carbon-14 dating.

MS. HOMES: So what about the present and the future?

MR. HENYEY: In geology, we say that the present is the key to the past. What we're saying really is that natural processes tend to be pretty much the same through geologic time. And so we're presuming things will happen at about the same rate in the future. Now, of course, these earthquakes don't come like clockwork, so obviously there are uncertainties that have to be accounted for. So when we say "predict" or "forecast," we have to do the same thing as the weather forecasters—you give a probability.

MS. HOMES: Do you have times when in your bones and in just your intuition, you think, oh, something's going to happen soon?

MR. HENYEY: Well, to some extent there are things that we're beginning to learn about earthquakes that are giving us some of these clues. Just to give an example, prior to the 1906 earthquake, between about 1850 and 1906, the number of moderate-sized earthquakes accelerated dramatically in northern California. These were the earthquakes in the magnitude range, let's say, of five and a half to six and a half. And then in 1906 we had almost an eight, it wasn't quite an eight but it was close. And then this intermediate size basically shut off. And it's now just beginning to pick up again. We have a very good sense now that really big earthquakes are preceded by intermediate-size earthquakes.

MS. HOMES: And how many of those? Is it ten of those or is it two of them?

MR. HENYEY: No, no. Maybe fifteen, twenty earthquakes. The idea in California is that the biggest earthquake we can have on a given fault is probably around a magnitude eight. Sort of like the 1906 earthquake. That's about the biggest one you've had in northern California. And in 1857 we had a pretty big one. It might not have been as big as we could have, but it approached the maximum size we think we could have in southern California. We don't think we can rupture the whole San Andreas because there are some strange things in the middle of it.

MS. HOMES: So how many of the mid-range earthquakes have we had?

MR. HENYEY: Well, we're starting to pick up on mid-range. 1857 was the last big one we had here in southern. Since 1952 moderate-size earthquakes have come more frequently in southern California than prior to 1952. So it may be that we're in this sort of accelerating phase now. The San Andreas is the guy that does this ultimate release of the stress. And we know that earthquakes on that fault take place on average about every hundred and fifty years, although the range is between maybe a hundred years and three or four hundred years, something like that.

MS. HOMES: Which is ... ?

MR. HENYEY: ... 2007 would be the average time. So we're already past kind of the lower bound, and we're reaching the midpoint now, or the average. But we still may have another fifty or a hundred years to go. So the fact that earthquakes maybe are picking up somewhat is not unusual.

MS. HOMES: How do we protect ourselves?

MR. HENYEY: Well, you build structures that are earthquake resilient. I mean a building like this one is sitting on a fault, it could be built to ride the thing out without it collapsing. There'd be total damage to the building if the fault cut through it, but what you want is, you want to build structures that aren't going to collapse, and that are going to suffer a minimum amount of damage, particularly those that aren't right on the fault.

MS. HOMES: I guess there's no such thing as an earthquake warning system.

MR. HENYEY: Well, in principle, we can give a few seconds of warning.

MS. HOMES: But what good is that?

MR. HENYEY: Well let's say we could give twenty seconds of warning, which we might be able to do. For example, if a major earthquake gets started on the San Andreas down near the Mexican border, and we have sensors down there and we can see it get started, we can send a radio signal or electronic telemetry signal from there to Los Angeles ... and you'd probably have twenty seconds, before the wave started arriving here.

MS. HOMES: Right.

MR. HENYEY: What you could do is you could stop elevators at the next floor and open the door and then cut off the elevators. You could stop trains. You could, in principle, put signals on bridges, and some of these big overpasses. A red light would go on and you'd have to stop, you couldn't get on one of these big overpasses. You could shut off gas lines. You could have automatic valves which immediately shut down gas lines or water lines, some of the key lines that feed into town. So there's a lot you could do. You couldn't protect the average person; in general, they'd still go about their business. But a lot of things you could do, which could save lives and save property.

MS. HOMES: Do you have any earthquake fears?

MR. HENYEY: Well, I guess I do, to some extent, in the

sense that you always wonder about the building you're in.

MS. HOMES: [laughing] Exactly! Do you live your life any differently for what you know about earthquakes?

MR. HENYEY: No, not really. The only thing I guess I did when I bought my house was I tried to get as far away from the San Andreas Fault as I possibly could and still be able to get to town, to USC, to work. But then I discovered I was on a fault, a very active fault. ... I didn't discover that until about twenty years after I bought my house.

MS. HOMES: Do you think people become progressively more afraid as they have more earthquakes?

MR. HENYEY: Well my feeling would be as people ride through earthquakes they become less concerned about them. You have to live here for a fairly long time, though, to ride out more than one major shake. And that's part of the problem, because people are continually moving about within the Los Angeles region. But I think if you've gone through several earthquakes, then you become more in tune with it, and begin to understand what they're all about. I mean, it certainly doesn't help to have an earthquake right under you. When that happens, I don't think people ever really learn to live with earthquakes comfortably.

MS. HOMES: Are there people who enjoy them? Like some great amusement park ride?

MR. HENYEY: Well, I must say I sort of enjoy them! [laughs] But I'm sure I wouldn't enjoy it if ...

MS. HOMES: If it was under your house!

MR. HENYEY: I think riding out an earthquake in California, if you're not in a very serious shaking zone, it's probably kind of a neat experience to a lot of people. Scientists will actually, if you start feeling the shaking, they'll start counting, thousand-one, thousand-two, thousand-three, because the first shaking is not as extreme as a little bit later. What happens is you have two major waves that start out at the same place, but one takes a little longer to get to you. One is called the P wave or Primary wave. And the other is called the S wave or Secondary wave. The Primary wave generally shakes you up and down, for the most part, whereas the Secondary wave is the one that shakes you back and forth. And that's the one that creates more damage. And so, it's just like two cars starting off at a stop light. One going twenty miles an hour, one going fifteen miles an hour. And when they've gone one block, one car's just a little ahead of the other. By the time they've gone a mile, the separation gets greater and greater. These two waves are just like those two cars, so you can tell how far away the earthquake is by what that separation is. And we know, roughly, from our experience, what ten seconds between those waves corresponds to in terms of distance, and so you can judge the distance of the earthquake. Once you judge the distance of the earthquake you can guess the magnitude. Let's say it takes twenty seconds between the two waves, you know it's probably something like a hundred kilometers away, and if it's shaking very strong, it's gotta be a pretty big earthquake.

CHAPTER FOUR

The Anthropology of the Every Day

I drive back from USC on the surface roads. I want to get a feel
for the city, to pace it out block by block. And then all of a sudden, on my right, at the intersection of Wilshire and Curson,
are the La Brea Tar Pits.

Before I'm even out of the car I smell the earthy brew of
asphalt, thick tar, a stench like gasoline, like heating oil—
heavy crude.

Despite the fact that everyone in L.A. has a car, or perhaps
because of it, it is incredibly easy to park just about everywhere.
There are meters on the streets, lots of parking lots and in the
absolute worst case—like in the middle of Beverly Hills—you
have to walk a couple of blocks.

I park right next to the tar pits. "There's really nothing to
see," a friend who lives in Los Angeles had said when I'd asked
her about them.

Rancho La Brea is one of the reasons I'm interested in Los Angeles. Right in the middle of the city are these active, bubbling pits, an inescapable reminder of not only the natural world, but the prehistoric, pre-Hollywood.

From New York when I thought of the words "tar pit," I imagined huge pits, like stone quarries, deep, bottomless. These pits, right by the side of the road, are more like pools. They're gleaming black oil slicks on L.A.'s Miracle Mile surrounded by palm trees and succulents. Fake Colombian mammoths in asphalt up to their ankles rise up out of the tar. The opposite of a zoo where the animals are real and the setting is fake, here the geography is real and the animals are a plastic fiction. And of course, there's a fence all around it. Admittedly it's a little disappointing if you're expecting huge frothing pits, but if you stand there for a couple of minutes, breathing the intoxicating fumes, watching, it becomes mesmerizing. Randomly, all around the pit, tiny geysers go off, eruptions like bursting blisters of bubbling crude break the surface, concentric circles of the stuff radiate out. "Oil, that is, black gold," to borrow a phrase from the opening song of the hit television series, *The Beverly Hillbillies*. The smell is strong, thick, black, sticky gasoline. One can almost imagine the vicious battles thousands of years ago, as saber-toothed tigers feasted upon horses trapped in the tar, while dire wolves looked on, and teratorn birds scavenged nearby. Just as I'm forcing my eyes to squint closed and bringing the faux mammoths to life, the sprinkler system kicks on—the sudden confusion between nature's eruptions and man's timed intrusions nearly gives me a heart attack.

Inside the museum, a set of windows overlooks a turtle pond. I overhear a mother excitedly explaining to one of the staff members that her family has a turtle that's gotten a little too big. She asks if the museum accepts local turtles. Her two little girls stand nearby, the elder seeming stricken that her mother is contemplating giving the family turtle away. "Sure," the man at the museum says, "we'd be happy to take your turtle. When do you want to bring him?"

"Well," the mother says, "I could go home and get it. I could bring it today."

The elder child looks to be on the verge of tears, filled with betrayal. This is not at all what she had in mind when she agreed to come to the museum. The oblivious mother finally picks up on how traumatic and unexpected this must seem. "Is that too soon?" the mother asks. "Do you need some time to say good-bye?"

The little girl nods, still speechless.

"You know," the man says to the little girl, "you can come and visit him any time you want. And he'll have a really good time with all the other turtles."

The girl, trying to be brave, nods.

"Great," the mother says, "I'll bring the turtle tomorrow."

The highlight of the museum is the paleontology lab where, through glass windows, you can watch people working to identify the various fossils recovered. The lab is filled with bones, with bits and pieces, with scientists seeming to work. While I'm there, one picks up a bone and shows it to another—presumably a visiting scientist (he's got a Visitor tag on his shirt). I'm the only one around watching through the glass. In front of each of the workstations is a homemade sign—I AM SORTING THE MATRIX OF THE SABER-TOOTHED CAT VERTEBRA. On each workstation is a container of picks, used toothbrushes, and other tools fashioned to clean the fossilized bones. Each worker seems to be vying for attention, begging to be watched.

The lab here reminds me of the tour of the FBI Building in Washington, D.C., where, in theory, you see FBI agents working to identify evidence. There, a sneaker sits on top of a desk, a plaster cast of the tread nearby. It is haunting, menacing. Did something happen to the other shoe? To the foot of the person wearing the sneaker? What can the sneaker tell us? The FBI tour, with no homemade signs, is less convincing. It's beyond unlikely the FBI would do its evidence-collecting and analysis in public view for tourists from around the world to watch—the real work is done behind closed doors at the lab in Quantico, Virginia.

At La Brea, every year from July to September you can visit the pits as they're being excavated and watch paleontologists recover bones from the saber-toothed tigers, fifteen-hundred-pound ground sloths, and dire wolves that died here thousands and thousands of years ago. Among the conclusions that the scientists have made is that the climate was wetter and cooler 28,000 years ago, and that many of the animals they've found ate a type of grass no longer found in the area—a grass that was dependent on summer rain.

From here I go on to a more modern archeological adventure: I go to Ralph's, the enormous grocery store on Sunset. We don't have grocery stores like this in New York—there isn't room. The Ralph's on Sunset is so big that it's not really a store but a working museum of American life. Here you'll find every product, every variation on every product, health foods, prepared foods, organic foods, frozen foods, dozens and dozens of kinds of milk, juice, soda, beer, and wine. I buy things I don't eat at home, Strawberry Pop-Tarts, knowing there is a toaster in the hotel room. I buy tea bags, orange juice, Coke, water. I go up and down the aisles, mesmerized. I go up and down thinking, didn't Joan Didion write an essay on Ralph's? Didn't Joan Didion write an essay on the horrible headache I have right now—the flying migraine I get every time I take a plane? Didn't Joan Didion write everything about Los Angeles that needed to be written, and if she didn't, Mike Davis did? I am having a moment of terrible doubt, of low blood sugar, the last thing I ate was the snack on the plane. In the candy aisle, I pick up a chocolate bar and eat it as I'm prowling. I feel both a lack of self-consciousness—I am so out of my element that I am invisible—and a certain self-doubt that being a total outsider I have no business attempting to make sense of this place. I am not from here; I don't know anything about here, I don't even know where "here" is.

"None of us know where we are," a woman in the cookie row spontaneously says. I look up to see who's talking. An older woman with thick gray hair stands in front of me, blocking my path. "You can get lost in a place like this," she says. "Any idea where they keep the frozens?"

"I'm always seeing those pictures in the supermarket papers," says Griffin Dunne. "Actresses who just pile in the car, they want to go to

Ralph's, and then these horrible pictures are taken of them. Because there really are people that hang out in Ralph's parking lot with telephoto lenses."

··········

One enters the Chateau Marmont through the garage—you drive in, drop off the car, go up a couple of steps, and make a right if you're going to one of the bungalows or a left if you're headed into the main building. The elevator goes all the way up, so there's no need to pass through the lobby, no need to stop at the front desk. This means if you want to be alone, you can be alone—it also means that a great place for spotting people is in the two chairs on the small patio between the main building and the garage, but in fact everyone is too cool to be seen just sitting there, waiting.

"And you would get on the elevator and there would be like the most historical and famous person in there. That's why it was kind of great," John Waters says. "And still when I come there I see all kinds of people. It's stars you'd want to meet!"

However, if you're looking for a little entertainment or a sociable snack, the lobby area is a lot like a living room filled with youthful, good-looking William Morris agents, courting their equally youthful, if more beautiful, clients. The clients lounge on overstuffed sofas while the agents lean forward in their club chairs, looking/leering at them, taking purposeful sips of their martinis before continuing to chart the course. From about 4:30 to 9:00 the lobby and courtyard are a kind of display case, a short course in how the young both date and do business in L.A.

The scale of the living room, the dark coziness of it, in contrast to the palm trees, the hard sun, outside, is relaxing. The room is always cool, cozy on even the hottest day and at night glows with the exotic, out-of-time, quasi-bordello lumens thrown off by the enormous Victorian lamps. Outside there is a colonnade with wicker chairs, large leafed plants, echoing of straw hats, strong cold drinks, and another time, almost tropical, almost deeply southern, and the prospect of dropping into a lovely late afternoon liquored sleep. The tan and brown awnings over the balconies flap in the breeze. With its European arches and architecture, the feel of the Chateau is so other, so starkly different from the Mondrian—otherwise known as the Mind Drain, where your name has to be on a list to get into their bar, and the bellhops routinely forget to deliver important messages. One time my rental car arrived and they forgot I had checked in and simply sent it back to Enterprise.

The Chateau, with its heavy beamed ceilings, moody wall sconces, and small tightly manicured front garden is a place where those who are so inclined sometimes erupt into impromptu improvisational modern dances across the grass.

Being at the Chateau is like being in a place that exists out of reality, a sacred place, like a church. And it is like not just any church, not just another California mission, it is *the* church—Our Los Angeles Lady of Creativity.

Jennifer Beals has a sort of theory about it. "In the United States, and especially in the West, there are so many structures that are devoid of any kind of history. So any time you walk into any structure that has any semblance of history, I think you start to feel the effect of all those other people who have been there. So I don't know whether it's by virtue of being on a vortex of energy, or whether that energy was created by virtue of all the people that have stayed there. But just walking into the lobby, you get the sense that you're part of a continuum. And you feel just really privileged to be part of that continuum. And you want to contribute to it in some way."

I am by the pool, prowling, when out of the corner of my eye, I see a man reading one of my books. It strikes me as strange. A waiter passes by; I ask him who's the man. He says he doesn't know who the man is but that the author of the book is someone who stays here a lot. "In fact, she was recently here," he says, as if letting me in on a secret. "He's reading the house copy, but we have it for sale upstairs as well."

"Thanks," I say, "I was just curious." I can't bring myself to tell him that it's me, that in fact I'm still here—I want to spare both of us the embarrassment.

I return to the lobby, take a seat in the living room area, and order a Cosmopolitan, even though I don't really drink. The Cosmo is a bit like rocket fuel with cranberry juice added for color—no wonder some people stay on these sofas all night. I love this room. I love just sitting here and watching. The lamps, which are turned on around dusk, are a deep antidote to minimalist cool. A couple that I know from New York, who happen to be staying at the hotel, join me on the sofa. We're having a nice conversation when a man sits in the empty club chair next to us. This is the hidden danger of vaguely communal seating groups, but usually people are self-conscious enough not to want to join a party to which they weren't invited.

"This seat taken?" the guy asks after he's already seated.

"It's yours," we say and then return to our conversation. He's clearly listening in. He nods along, we try to ignore him. As we talk, he plunges himself into our conversation, offering his commentary on the subject we're discussing—British ex-patriots. Within moments, he has changed the subject entirely; we are now talking about him, about the script for a pilot that he's working on. He keeps interrupting himself to make hostile references to his wife. At a certain point I ask if he's staying at the hotel. He says, yes, he's been here for several months, in a bungalow out back. He's been brought out here to do some sort of a rewrite. I ask if he's here with the wife. He mentions that his wife is the author of a kind of handbook for nerdy types hoping to improve themselves. He says they're recently separated. And while he could well have had a wife who wrote such a book, he is the kind of crazy who scares me most—the kind who doesn't seem to know he's crazy. At a certain point he offers a copy of his script—he'll just run to his room and get it. He leaves. We talk about him behind his back, we speculate that he's not exactly for real. The gentleman among us is annoyed—we should give him the benefit of the doubt. He returns a few minutes later, hardly huffing and puffing, and hands me his script.

"Thanks, I can't wait to read it."

I glance at one page. The only thing on the page is the word "you." You. All the way down the page, written as dialogue, one "You" per line, fifteen lines each attributed to a specific character. It would be Mametesque except that it's not. I turn the page—"Suck," again all the way down the page, fifteen lines, each attributed to a character. "You Suck."

"Looks interesting."

I am now afraid of the document I am holding. I am afraid of the person sitting before me and worse, he knows who I am. He knows that I am actually staying in the hotel.

"Well," I say, checking my watch, excusing myself, winking at my friends. "I'd better get back to it—expecting that conference call any minute now. I'll call you later."

On my way to the elevator I stop at the front desk.

"See that guy sitting over there?" I say. The clerk comes out from behind the desk and takes a good look. He nods.

"Is he staying here?"

"Nope, I don't think so."

"Well, he thinks he is. He thinks he's been living here for several months, in a bungalow. You might want to keep an eye out. He gave me this. I show him *You Suck*.

"I'll let the security guy know."

I nod. And take the elevator up.

When I think of living at a hotel, I think of Eloise at the Plaza, Nabokov coming for a visit at Le Montreux Palace in 1961 and finding it so much to his liking that he stayed until he died in his suite at the hotel in 1977. I think of how exotic and fashionable it is to call the Carlyle or the Sherry-Netherland in New York home. I think of Dorothy Parker and Robert Benchley holding court at their Algonquin Round Table. I think of parties, the high life, jet-setters coming and going, shopping bags, room keys, bellhops, porters, housekeepers, room service waiters, telephone operators, night auditors, house doctors, overnight shoe shines, morning papers just outside your door, the gentle tap, tap of breakfast arriving at a preappointed hour.

"You feel you're in a private club," says photographer Todd Eberle. "You feel you're richer than you are—it's so glamorous, just driving up, from the neon sign to the Gucci billboard over the pool to the striped awnings, and it's got incredible charm."

CHAPTER FIVE

On the Eighth Day

My message light is blinking. It's Dr. Fred Kogen, the mohel of Beverly Hills, returning my call. I'd heard about him from friends in New York, who'd recently returned from a bris in Beverly Hills.

"If you're going to L.A., you have to meet this guy," they said. "He does all the big circumcisions. No pun intended. He has his own website. Here's the web address, his phone number, and his cell phone. If you're looking for people to talk to about L.A.—this is your guy. He is L.A."

"I'm flattered," Dr. Kogen said when I called him back, after I told him how highly he'd been recommended. "Can you come here? How's tomorrow morning?"

"Sounds good, Dr. Kogen."

"If you keep calling me Dr. Kogen, I'm not going to talk to you anymore—my name is Fred."

"Yes, Dr. Kogen, I mean Fred," I said as I scribbled down the instructions to his Woodland Hills home.

I set out first thing in the morning, and take a long winding ride from my spot on Sunset Boulevard up into Woodland Hills. The exterminator arrives just as I do—smoking a big cigar. As Dr. Kogen and I settle into the living room, I cannot escape the surreality of watching the exterminator through the picture window, walking around with a gas mask on, pumping toxins into the air.

"Ants," Kogen says. "I have really bad ants."

Kogen is an affable guy—a few years back he was named one of *Cosmopolitan* magazine's most eligible bachelors. At the moment, he's exhausted, tousled—he's just gotten up. His schedule has him running to all ends of the state, performing seven to ten brisses a week—there's a lot of baby boys being born in California. After asking if I'd like coffee or tea, he brings out a pot of green tea for himself, pouring it into a small blue and white china tumbler. Ceremony is important to Kogen. We sit discussing the ancient rites of circumcision as practiced in modern day Los Angeles and what it means to be a mohel in the year 2001. We talk about his website, contemporary spirituality, and about the big issues in circumcision—the use of local anesthetic as well as the importance of holding a good parking place for the mohel just outside the house (emergency supplies are kept in the car). It is only long after we're done and I'm back at the hotel that I realize I forgot to ask him what he does with the foreskins.

MS. HOMES: How did you become a doctor?

DR. KOGEN: I went to the University of Illinois at Champaign for undergrad. I'm from Chicago. My mother raised me alone in a one-bedroom apartment—very middle-class. People, when they meet me, assume that I'm from a similar background as most of the clientele out here. They're usually second-generation nouveaux riches. I paid every dime, loans, the whole thing. I worked as a waiter. I was always very proud of my Jewish heritage. And I came out here as a resident in 1984; I was training at Cedar Sinai, all excited to be in L.A., gynecologist to the stars, the whole deal. Doing my residency I'd see these guys who were fifty years old, with ten patients in a row. I didn't love it that much that I'm going to be wanting to get out of bed every morning and roll into the hospital.

MS. HOMES: Right.

DR. KOGEN: So, I wasn't sure what I was going to do. Meanwhile, someone who was a few years ahead of me started the first training program outside of the state of Israel to train doctors or nurse practitioners, who already knew how to do a circumcision, to be a mohel. And they were looking to actively train individuals who were in the doctor community. They said, you're new in L.A., you're Jewish, and you're single, you do a nice circumcision, and if you get in the community you'll meet a nice Jewish woman. And I thought, you know what, this is a kick. I'll put it on my résumé, it will be a good time for me, so I took the training class. I was in the second class. At the time there were only eight of us in the country. I was the youngest physician mohel at the time. I was twenty-six years old when I completed the program. We were terrified. In some ways more terrified than if my life was actually in danger. I couldn't have been more nervous.

MS. HOMES: Did you ever think of becoming a rabbi?

DR. KOGEN: No, but people have suggested that to me several times. What's interesting is that I didn't have such a strong religious background. I'd feel uncomfortable, I'd want to leave the bris right away because I feared people would ask me questions. But I'll never forget my first bris. First of all, do I charge them? Is that fair? I've never done one before. And secondly, do I tell them this is my first bris? So the first call came in—they got me off the list from the temple. And they didn't bother asking how long I've been doing this, how many have I done, they just said show up. I said fine. And then came the next question, what's your fee? Well, I had to charge them a minimal amount, so I charged them the minimal amount. I show up and, much to my consternation, I walk into a room filled with macho Israeli guys and an Israeli family. I was twenty-six at the time, and I was thinner and younger and I happened to look young for twenty-six. And these guys immediately surrounded me. And they're all laughing. You're the doctor! And the mohel! You are too young to be a doctor and mohel! What is this, your first bris? And they're all laughing. I go, "As a matter of fact, it is!" They thought I was laughing because I was joking. I was laughing because I was so terrified. I was shaking so much during the circumcision, I had to keep my elbow in my stomach just to steady my hand. Afterwards, immediately they said, you want a drink? Yeah, I'd like a shot of vodka! It was a terrifying experience. It takes years to really become competent. Because, as opposed to a residency where you're following an established doctor, your professor, and there's a constant patient flow where you get to kind of hone your skills, as a mohel, there's nothing like that. Six months later I'm in a big mansion in Bel Air and everyone there is an attorney from Beverly Hills, and the grandparents insist on telling me they're all attorneys, you better not screw up, and there are three rabbis there who flew in from New York. And half of them are producers and directors. And I was terrified.

MS. HOMES: What do you do when you're terrified?

DR. KOGEN: Well, there's nothing you can do. You've got to go for it, unless you quit. I had a colleague who was an obstetrician gynecologist in Beverly Hills, and she was performing her first bris ... she's ready to do the actual cut, and she reaches over and notices that she forgot the scalpel blade. And she stops everything, goes in her bag, and starts looking around in there, and brought no blade. They had to take scissors, or a knife from the kitchen, and do the final cut. And she said, that was it. She came back three times, four times, made sure the baby didn't get infected, and never did a bris again. It's just terrifying. Because most doctors are used to doing an operation in a hospital, which is a very secure, comfortable setting. They have a lot of backup, they close the door, they're in the operating suite, they want more light, less light, music. They want some extra hands, grab an extra nurse, more supplies, move the table up, move the table down, change the lighting, give me hot or cold, is it hot in here, too cold? I'll tell you something. A bris can be an unbelievably powerful thing, and I get letters from families who say that they'll never forget it. If it's done with the right attitude—it can be a powerful, wonderful experience.

MS. HOMES: One of the things you were saying before was how it really is a sort of bloodletting, tribal, male-bonding thing.

DR. KOGEN: It absolutely is, if you step back and look at the essence of it. It is a bloodletting. It is something that has been done, prior to the Jews, by African tribes and cultures. Egyptians, Phoenicians, used to do it on adolescents. And even the Muslims, in the first year, and usually between the ages of nine and thirteen. And clearly it's a bloodletting. It's tribal. It identifies you as born into the tribe. What's remarkable about it is here we are, year 2001, the beginning of the millennium, and we're performing something that is thousands of years old ... in context. More importantly, in context in L.A. Where much is cutting-edge.

MS. HOMES: No pun intended!

DR. KOGEN: No pun intended. I'm sorry. Cutting-edge cultural, fashion, media, everything. Convenience. Los Angeles, in many ways, is the genesis point for the world. And here I am, with the people who are working in this area. And not just L.A., San Francisco. I'm taking care of half the people at Oracle. But yet, when we get down to it, I'll be doing a bris at the Beverly Hills Hotel, at the Four Seasons Hotel, the owners of the hotel are there, it's their grandchild. Everyone is as polished, as refined, and as elegant, as worldly and as sophisticated as possible. There are hundreds of people showing up, limousines pulling up, valet parking, full catered event, live band, orchestra, everything else. And we're all sitting around, standing around this poor little baby, cutting off the end of his penis. It's unbelievable! It really is unbelievable!

MS. HOMES: One of the things you talked about before was that sometimes you're doing this for a family that isn't a Beverly Hills family. How would you describe the difference between the two?

DR. KOGEN: The ceremonies that I like best have nothing to do with the theatrical or the people, in terms of their financial status or their power status. To me it is purely the essence of the family themselves. If it's a loving, emotionally-connected, respectful ceremony, respectful of themselves, their child, and me— because sometimes they're actually quite disrespectful to me and what I'm trying to accomplish—then I'm thrilled. I don't care who they are, as long as the ceremony rises to the point that I hope it rises to. I look at myself as the person who lays the foundation. I do the best I can, I work hard at it. I'm very passionate about how it should be. I speak to people on the phone for hours, and I try to guide them to make the ceremony a thoughtful ceremony, but I can only go so far.

MS. HOMES: What would be an example of their not being respectful? They're just not getting the significance of it?

DR. KOGEN: Here's a kind of interesting example of the difference between quote, the more middle-class or more average individual versus the more sophisticated and wealthy. I find that in general, the people who are more average—more average, that's such a poor term, I don't really like that term—they tend to spend more time and energy and more emotional focus on the one-on-one, and what the needs are to do a safe and proper ceremony. I find that those who are in the more upper echelons spend much more time worrying about the caterer, the setting, flower arrangements, renting the tables, and making sure that the bar is well stocked. So I would show up to a multimillion-dollar mansion in Bel Air, and even though I've talked to these people over and over again, and they've reassured me they'll take care of my needs, and I walk in ... and nothing I asked for has been taken care of. However, I look around, and they've got the caterer running around setting up, they've got a full staff. So it's not as though they don't have the money or the wherewithal to get someone to help them follow my instructions, they just don't take what I need seriously. And it changes my whole mood. At that point I become the angry mohel. I find that that's much less common in the more average family;

they really follow my instructions and take it to heart. Sometimes I wonder why the extremely wealthy individuals even do it. They do it because they feel it's necessary, but there seems to be no connection to it.

MS. HOMES: Are they less spiritual, or less religious, do you think?

DR. KOGEN: I think in terms of the central connection to the emotional element of it, sometimes they seem more disconnected. I don't know what comes first, the chicken or the egg. Whether or not they are the more successful ones because they have that emotional disconnect, or they become more emotionally disconnected as they become more successful. … You know, the entertainers, especially in this town, they get an award for everything. I mean everyone's kissing their tuchus. They're performing something and I'm thinking, they have twenty million takes, they can do it over and over again, different angles. They've got a support structure up the wazoo, painting them and coloring them and lighting them and this and that. They've got the teleprompters. And as a mohel, there's none of that. And there's no reward. There's no Christmas; Hanukkah time we get our apples or our gifts. There's no awards banquet, there's no retirement banquet. There's none of that. I have another issue, particularly in this town. I get a phone call from the assistant.

MS. HOMES: Right.

DR. KOGEN: "Hi, this is Larry, I'm so-and-so's assistant. Are you Dr. Kogen?" Yes. "Well, so-and-so's having a baby, and they would like you to be the mohel at the bris. We have it scheduled ..." They already have it scheduled. They don't even know if I'm available and I can do it, but they've already taken care of it. And then I'll say okay, and who's so-and-so, and then they'll give me the name, and I say well, okay, and I do the paperwork. I'm filling out the database with their name, just like a medical report, and saying, What do they do? And basically you hear a pause, and then you hear ... "[breathes deeply] Well, they happen to be the president of Columbia TriStar," or whatever. And I'll say, "You know, in all due respect, Larry, if they're not a rabbi, I don't know who they are!" Why would I know them? And that always becomes a nightmare, because the assistants protect their clientele. I asked one family, you want me to circumcise the kid, what's the address? And they said, we can't give that out. And I said first of all it's a medical chart, nobody's going to see this, I'm not going to put this on CNN. And second of all, I'm supposed to go there. So when I'm there, don't you think I'll know where it is? It's classic. So I've performed ceremonies in eight states. I get flown to Vegas quite often. I've performed on tennis courts, with red carpets, live band, live music, professional photographer, professional videographers. And also, I've given a bris where they were deaf, they had to sign it all the whole time. I've done brisses for interfaith, inter-race, single moms, I've had families who are gay males, two gay males. Interfaith gay males, who mixed their semen together in a test tube and inseminated a straight mom.

MS. HOMES: Are there ever moments when you're doing it, you think, Oh God, this isn't going well, and you sort of wish everybody wasn't watching?

DR. KOGEN: The circumcision?

MS. HOMES: Yeah.

DR. KOGEN: No, not at this stage.

MS. HOMES: How many do you think you've done at this point?

DR. KOGEN: Approximately four thousand.

MS. HOMES: So you've kind of got it down by now.

DR. KOGEN: Recently I did a bris for a family. They lived in this unbelievable house in Beverly Hills. The father of the baby lived at his grandparents' house. He was an architect in Mexico City, and he designed the home, and all these people flew in from Mexico City, and the Jews there are generally very, very wealthy, and the home was enormous. Just one of those unbelievable homes—I've been in a few, that's what's great about my job. It's really incredible. There's nothing quite like it. You have to understand something, it's the only operation that's an elective operation, not emergency, where a stranger comes in and thirty minutes later he's doing it. Usually you know your doctor, you have an established relationship before the operation. In my case, I don't meet these people. I walk in the door, and they're handing me the most precious thing in the world, and I'm operating on it! On his penis! And all the issues that come with it. One father said to me, "My son's going through this, I was wondering, before we get started and go out there, can you stick a needle in my penis, because I want to bond with my son, I want to feel the same thing." And his wife just kind of looked at me like "Oh, another day with my husband. No big deal." So he dropped his drawers. I said, "Come on, we gotta get going!" Took his penis, stuck a needle in it, pulled his drawers back up, packed up, and did the bris! So you know, it's amazing. And that's what I like about my work, is that I'm always in a new home, a new place. The traffic is terrible, horrible—that's killing me. I'll end up doing brisses in places like Modesto, Fresno, or southern Orange County, San Diego, I'll do three ceremonies and then I'll jump in a plane.

MS. HOMES: Have you had parents faint?

DR. KOGEN: I haven't had parents faint. I've had other people pass out. Oh, I can tell you stories, funny stories about that. How many stories do you want?

MS. HOMES: Well, I'm almost out of time.

DR. KOGEN: There's a lot to talk about. Do you want to meet again? I can make time. Do you want to go to a bris?

CHAPTER SIX

Do You Need to Be Validated?

The easiest way to be in Los Angeles is to be here for work—it gives you a focus, something to do. I decide that while I am here, I should do a little work, L.A. style. I need a new film agent. I make a list of who I'm interested in and make a few calls.

The initial decisions about who I'll meet are based upon how quickly my initial call is returned—in L.A. anything over twenty minutes is not acceptable unless the person is under general anesthesia. And then on the follow-up—do they have any idea of who I am? Do they pronounce my name correctly? Do they call me A. M. or Anne? Do they ask what the A. M. stands for? And when the assistant faxes directions to the office, is my last name spelled correctly—without an "L"? It's a set of basic indicators, but by no means definitive.

The meetings go like this: The receptionist buzzes the agent's assistant to tell them that I'm here. "It'll just be a minute," the receptionist says. "Would you like something to drink?"

"No thanks," I say and sit down in one of the black leather chairs. It is like the waiting room of an upscale outpatient surgery center—not only can we represent you, but we can also do a nice colonoscopy.

The agent's assistant comes out and introduces himself. The assistants are almost always male and almost always have a one-syllable name, Brad. Tad. Sad.

If it's a really big, high-end agency, the walls and corridors are covered with art, good art. I stop to look, recognizing most of the pieces immediately—the best of contemporary. "Interesting," I say to the assistant as I'm being led down the hall. "That's a Gregory Crewdson from his last show." "Really," Tad, Brad, Lad says, "how do you know that?" "I know the artist," I say, "and that's a Nan Goldin, and a Cindy Sherman, and a really nice Gursky." "Wow," the assistant says, his head whipping around as though I've sprayed the place with machine-gun fire. The assistant shows me into an empty room; either a spare office or conference room. "He's just on a call and will be right with you—would you like something to drink? Coffee, water, Diet Coke?"

"Fine, water then, thanks," I say.

The agent comes in. I'm Bob, or Ben, or Jonathan, and this is part of my team. Do you mind if Amanda, Jennifer, or Jersey sits in with us? The above named are young people, earnest, Ivy League but bottom of the class (with good connections). They come in carrying legal pads. They carry the pads as if they like the feel of carrying a legal pad, as if they like the words, "legal pad." It makes them think they might be in law school, that they might have gotten into law school—if they'd applied. Throughout the meeting they take notes and never speak.

The agent begins.

"I read about your book."

"I read the reviews of your book."

"I heard I should read your book."

"Your book agent is fantastic, I love him."

"What does your book agent say about me?"

"Does he know you're here?"

"Who do we have in common?"

"Six degrees, always six degrees."

"Do I see you in this business?"

"Are you willing to stop being a novelist to come out to California and live? Are you willing to give up everything and become one of us?"

"Are you crazy?"

"Do I look crazy?"

"We're all crazy, that's what we're doing here."

The agent performs and then he stops and waits for the applause.

"So, whadda ya think?"

I begin again, in another agency with another agent, in another office. This time it's entirely a solo show.

"Let me tell you about you."

"Let me tell you about myself."

"Is there anything you want to ask me?"

"Anyone you want to know?"

"Do you know who I work with?"

"Do you know what they think of me?"

"I'm not trying to sell myself to you, we're past that; you and I, we're the same person, the same thing. You and I, we're it, we're in this together. You and I," he says, gesturing like an ape, going back and forth banging his chest, pointing at my face, pointing his fingers directly into my face like he's about to poke out my eyes. "I want you to meet people. I want you to do well, if you do well then I do well. I'm the guy you want calling people. You want to know why, because I'll call them, I'll call them every day and I won't take no for an answer. And you know what else, people are happy to hear from me. They know it's not bullshit when I call. They know I represent the best, the fact that you're my writer means something. You may not know that, but they do. Here it's all about who you know and what you sell and what you've got. And they all want what you've got. You've got the one thing they don't have and can't just get anywhere—you've got talent."

I try again, elsewhere.

"What can you do for me?" an agent says, and I wonder if he's really asking or if it's a rhetorical question. "What can we do for you? What can you do for me that I can't do for myself, that's the question you should be asking," he says. "Well, we can set you up, we can put you in a room with people. You're special, you're different, you're what they want, you're the thing they're looking for, even if they don't know it yet. Even if they don't know who you are, don't worry about that—that's my job. Not everyone here is a reader; we've got to tell you that, but your reputation, your name alone is recognizable. You're the kind of person they love—a smart novelist from New York, but remember they might be a little scared of you. Our job is to let people know who you are, to prepare them, to lubricate the system. Your job is to come up with ideas—do you have any ideas?"

"Have you written anything?" another agent asks.

"Do you want to write for a TV show, do you want a staff position, because if that's what you want, if that's what would do it for you, if you'd be willing to move to L.A., I can do that for you, I can get that for you right now while you're sitting in that chair. I can pick up the phone and it can happen, over and out, a done deal. What do you say—wanna sign?"

One of the agents I meet with is a young guy with an office in Beverly Hills. We walk out together—it's the end of the day. We take the elevator down to the underground garage. The garage guy pulls his car around.

"Nice meeting you," I say, shaking his hand. "Great car."

"You like it?" he says, "I'm ready to sell it, do you want it?"

"No, thanks."

"Low mileage, still under warranty, it's a Beemer, for chrissake."

I shake my head. The valet pulls up in my white Ford Focus.

"Why don't you want to buy my car?" the agent whines. "It's certainly better than that."

"This is a rental," I say. "Remember, I don't live here."

"I think you should buy my car. If you bought it you would live here and I would get you work. Buy my car and you will be rich."

"What is it, like a magic genie lamp?"

"Hey, all I do is drive it on the freeway. It's good miles, highway miles."

I get into my Ford Focus. "Have a nice day," I say because I can't think of anything else to say.

He calls the next morning, "I just wanted to follow up, not so much about the meeting, you should do what feels comfortable, but about the car—are you going to buy my car?"

After every meeting, just as I'm leaving, the receptionist says to me loudly—"Do you need to be validated?" And I think this is what they do to detoxify you after these encounters. The receptionist, the lowest person on the totem pole, sees you on your way out and says a bunch of nice things to make you feel better, to make you feel like it's not really all that strange.

I look at her blankly—Do I need to be validated? I'm tempted to say more, I'm tempted to say, no frankly I'm fine, I'm really quite all right, but all of you really seem to need to be validated, seem to need a lot of attention, a lot of recognition. Everywhere I go, all of these talent agencies, all they do is ask—Do I need to be validated? It's pathetic.

"Your parking?"

"I'm doing what?"

"Your parking ticket—do you need your parking ticket validated?"

"You mean, all along I've been paying for parking? I've been paying to come to these meetings, I've been drinking your lousy bottles of water, thinking, well at least I should get something out of it and all along I could have been parking for free? God, what an idiot."

"Don't feel bad about it," the receptionist says, "you're not from here."

"That's right," I say, slapping my ticket down on the counter—"validate me."

CHAPTER SEVEN

Desert Oasis or Dry Spell?

I am only in Los Angeles for a couple of days and then I do what every one does—I leave. Already it is too much. The phone has been ringing like crazy—strangers, friends of friends all calling, offering me their Los Angeles, the real Los Angeles, the better Los Angeles. It's become a competition—the actor's Los Angeles, the realtor's Los Angeles, the immigrant's Los Angeles, the artist's Los Angeles, the magician's Los Angeles, and each is entirely interesting and a world unto itself, but I am reminding myself, as well as my callers, that I am not writing the bible of Los Angeles, that in fact I am the most unlikely person to be writing about Los Angeles at all—I'm not even sure I like Los Angeles.

I get in the car—grateful that I never really unpacked, that I'm able to pull myself together with fire-drill swiftness. I take off for the desert, imagining I am moving like a cartoon character, I am moving like Road Runner, hightailing it out of town, like Fred Flintstone, feet sticking out from under the car, getting a running start.

It is cold and raining and that's one of the things that no one wants to talk about—the unnamed season. In other parts of the country, all over the world, it's called winter, but in L.A. they insist they have no winter.

My plan is to drive into the desert, take a couple of days and collect my thoughts. After all, California is about cars, about driving, about long overlapping highways. I am in the car, on the road, and I begin to notice there's absolutely nothing interesting about the drive. It is all highways, connective tissue, dotted with shopping malls, car dealerships, mini storage facilities, and suburban housing developments. There is nothing interesting about any of it except that wherever I go— gas station, coffee shop—the wind blows icy rain in my face and every person between the hotel and Palm Springs apologizes, "This never happens here." "I don't know what's got into the weather, it's that global storming thing." "What can I tell you, we all have bad days."

Even the desert—which I imagine as hot and baking, which I imagine as desolate and lonely with long stretches of empty road and hawks circling over the car—is crowded, cold, and wet.

I am here during the energy crisis of 2001, Pacific Gas and Electric is declaring bankruptcy, there is the threat of a Writers Guild strike, followed by the threat of an Actors Guild strike, and the entrepreneurial explosion in Silicon Valley technology is starting to look like nuclear fallout as dot-com and tech stocks implode. Rolling blackouts sweep across the counties and in general the Golden State isn't exactly looking buff and sunshiny at the moment.

In most of Los Angeles when you talk to people about energy, about the need to conserve energy, they take it personally, not in the same way that they take recycling personally, making sure the newspapers and the plastics get out to the curb, but personally in that they think you are referring to their own energy level—their personal energy. "I have to conserve—my trainer comes to me, my yogaist comes to me, my masseuse comes to me—that way I'm not living in the car, not wasting time."

It is about doing what comes easiest, it is about the lifestyle, about living life the way you imagine it should be— Los Angeles is so much about fantasy that it constantly verges on breaking from reality. "I'm going to wait until my planets align before I make any big decisions," someone confesses to me poolside at the hotel.

"Are you a guest here at the Chateau?"

"No," she says, "I live down the street; I'm crashing."

The drive from Los Angeles to Palm Springs is unremarkable until, coming up over a hill, heading into the Coachella Valley, I see something amazing. At first I'm not even sure what I'm seeing. Graceful, elegant, like twenty-first century prehistoric fabrications, like long necked swans, like dinosaurs, one hundred and twenty, one hundred and forty, and two hundred feet high, they are windmills—in a postapocalyptic landscape. With blades like airplane propellers, each windmill spins at its own speed and some not at all. A stunningly conceptual installation, these oddly beautiful, man-made machines stand tall against the increasingly unearthly ground beneath.

The story of the Coachella Valley is the tale of an ancient ocean, a river that overflowed, and a lake that rose above sea level and emptied back into the river. This is where the Pacific and North American continental plates meet—the San Andreas Fault cuts right through the valley. And it is the story of the Native Americans who lived here—the Cahuilla tribes still in existence—the Spanish explorers and the coming of the railroads and the pioneers, all of which happened long before the rich and famous discovered it and seemed to think they'd found someplace new, someplace just for themselves.

The windmills belong to Wintec Energy, a wind farm. Utilities lease the land from the owners, buy the equipment, and set up. On this farm there are nine companies operating different variations of windmills.

As wind sucks through the pass and into the Coachella Valley, the wind machines take a bite out of it, and then farther down another set of blades takes another bite, all of it dependent on nature—on a wind season from February to September, all of it renewable, clean, regenerating.

It is about aerodynamic lift—the same thing that makes airplanes fly, the very thing that terrifies me. The idea that the technology that ground grain and pumped water in ancient China and spun the cloth sails of the Dutch tower mills of the 1400s is now producing the electricity that lets me turn my computer on and off is thrilling. I stand watching the transformation of air into electricity, watching as the pitch of the blades varies, as a breeze is turned into megawatts. Knowing that electricity can't be stored—it needs to be constantly manufactured—I am awed by the effort.

There are public tours of the wind farm, which give a history of the technology and then a ride out into the fields. I get a private tour, a wonderful rich explanation of the wind, of the issues in wind farming, and a history of the Coachella Valley itself.

In a truck we ride out to the field; rain splashes hard on the windows and roof. "Sorry about this," the fellow who's taking me on the tour says. "Sorry about the weather, it's not usually like this."

We are in a valley with hills all around, rocky, hard-packed dirt/sand—the Earth's crust—is the floor of the field. The tall towers surround us and the fellow is explaining the process through which the wind is actually transformed into power.

"Step out if you want," he says. I open the door, not knowing there is something more. The sound is overwhelming, like seagulls or whales, haunting, mystical, magical—a kind of mournful hollow bleating, seesawing squeaky call and response. This is the sound of air being bitten by blades; it is sexy and profound. If it weren't raining I could stand here forever. For the first time all day, there is something wonderful about the rain, the unrelenting grayness, and the weight of the sky, something wonderful about the sound of man and nature mating in the desert.

The wind farm makes other kinds of farming look silly; apple orchards look like kid stuff. The guys who work here couldn't be nicer, more patient, as they attempt to explain everything to me—the California power grid, transformers, gears, turbines, laminar flow. They invite me to lunch, but I decide I'd better get on with it—I've got places to go and besides I'm shivering now.

Someone in the gift shop—and of course there is a gift shop, this is America, after all—overhearing that I'm interested in the history of the Coachella Valley, says, "Well, it's the methamphetamine capital of the world. All these boys are in their basements with barrels of who knows what cooking up, a batch of the recipe, the hooch that burns your brain."

Thanks for sharing.

I leave the wind farm and head into Palm Springs. If you paint it gold they will come. As a hotel fanatic, I've been looking forward to what comes next: Merv Griffin's Resort Hotel and Givenchy Spa. High luxury, the best of Palm Springs, the descriptions in its literature make it sound great.

All day, in this rainy raw land, I've been dreaming of a long hot bath and a treatment of some sort, a massage, reflexology, or maybe even something a little more unusual, like the hot stone experience I keep seeing in spa catalogs. I will give myself a gift, in an attempt to seduce myself into telling the story of California's physical culture—hands-on.

Maximum pampering is how the spa describes itself, offering the standard treatments and newer things like watsu— where you are held in a pool of water and the therapist moves your body in various gentle, relaxing, stretching ways. After driving for hours, it sounds incredibly good—and I'm already sopping wet.

From the moment I arrive, the staff seems surprisingly

uninterested in my need for a "treat." I pull into the driveway and it takes ten minutes before I can find someone to take the car.

The main building is faux gaudy, celebrating excess but not even real excess—rather, it's perceived excess, excess for those who don't see very well anymore, for those who mistake the color yellow for gold leaf. The spa building is a cross between the White House and a European villa.

There is a strange culture in Palm Springs, a culture without culture, a blending of all styles and aesthetics where the organizing idea is that everything colored gold is good. It is also a town of retired decorators, of men who call themselves boys, men who are obsessed with and constantly celebrating that most boyish part of themselves, men who prefer the company of other boys who even at fifty, sixty, and seventy are happy to be referred to as boys. Gay retirees are in many ways the lifeblood of this town. Conservative, closeted (only in that they never told their parents), they congregate in the local antique shops among objects of gold—gilded mirrors, fountains with boys peeing. The gay women, a slightly wilder and younger set, descend annually for the Dinah Shore golf tournament and for drinking and topless dancing by the pool. For whatever reason, there has long been a measure of acceptance of gays in this otherwise deeply conservative insider's outside place. There is also a large community of swingers—you know, wife swappers. Just a few years ago the annual Lifestyles Convention was held in Palm Springs, and the local devotees regularly gather for a barbecue and what can only be described as a sex fest. All over the town there are "gay" guest houses and clothing-optional motels and resorts that advertise "single women welcome" and "Playroom," meaning sex dens for swinging couples looking for action.

Either way, it's still raining at Merv Griffin's. I check in and am shown to my room. It's a golf cart ride away from the main building, where the spa facilities and restaurants are. It looks out over a parking lot and has a notably low ceiling. All this can be yours for four hundred twenty-five dollars a night.

"Wow," I say, otherwise at a loss for words. Before the bellman brings the bags up, I am on the phone to the front desk. "What else have you got?" I hold while the manager flips through the "pages" of his computer.

I look out onto the parking lot—even the cars aren't terribly interesting or luxurious. The whole facility—the low-key two-story buildings, the ubiquitous golf carts—reminds me of a retirement facility, of assisted living.

As I step out into the hall, the door across the way opens and a worker comes out holding a tank, a green pressurized canister, like something a scuba diver might carry or an exterminator, with two hoses and a gauge.

"Freon," the man says to me.

Just beyond him in the center of the room, an older woman sits sternly upright in a chair, reading a book. How often do you see a woman, sitting by herself, in the middle of the afternoon in a hotel room, reading? There's something about the sight of her and the man with the freon canister that allows my mind to conflate the two, that lets me for half a second think that the worker was in the room, filling the woman with freon, helping her maintain the crisp chill of the vegetable bin, as she sharply turns the pages.

The door closes.

The second room they show me is worse than the first—it's like a Motel 6 on steroids, massive furniture, tasteless, but no doubt expensive. It reminds me of the kind of high-end, but ugly, furnishings my grandparents had in their apartment in Coral Gables, Florida. And it is dark, very dark. My aesthetic allergies are kicking in big-time; my stomach is growling.

I pick up the phone again and apologetically excuse myself from the hotel register. "It's not what I expected, not what I had in mind. Unfortunately, I'll need to check out, immediately." Within thirty minutes I have had the full Merv Griffin's Resort and Givenchy Spa experience.

As my bags are golf-carted back to the main building, I wait and chat with the bellhop. I ask if he's ever been to the wind farm. "Amazing, isn't it?" I say.

"Incredible," he says. "an eyesore, a blot on the landscape."

From my cell phone, I call the next stop on my itinerary, La Quinta Resort and Club, and ask if they can accommodate me a day early. I drive there, reminding myself of the sound of the windmills, the baleful bleating of wind turned to wine.

La Quinta is one of a few towns named for a hotel. The hotel itself, built in 1926 as an ersatz fountain of youth, offered desert sun, quiet, privacy. It quickly became a favored Hollywood retreat—Greta Garbo liked it here, as did Joan Crawford, Marlene Dietrich, Katharine Hepburn, Errol Flynn, Clark Gable. Frank Capra came here to write *It Happened One Night*. He thought of it as an incredibly lucky place and returned to write several other films, including *Mr. Smith Goes to Washington*.

La Quinta incorporated in 1981 and is among the fastest-growing cities in California. And the La Quinta resort is no longer just a desert hideaway, it's one of the prime spots for high-end business conferences. The last time I was here, one of the largest brokerage houses was holding its annual conference on technology. The CNBC trucks were there, satellites up, broadcasting live. Watching it all on cable TV from my room, I had the strange sensation of seeing some sort of closed-circuit, on-site surveillance channel. It's a peculiar experience to think you've escaped for a few days of deep R & R and then right there outside your window, and in fact your window itself on certain occasions, is being broadcast live around the world—welcome to the twenty-first century. As I watched, both in person and on the tube, the heads of major companies made their appearances, names like Jobs, McNeeley, Ellison. Between sessions, the plaza was flooded with the best of minds on cell phones, working their two-way pagers, sucking down warm chocolate chip cookies, freshly popped popcorn, and Häagen Dazs bars, all of it being handed out right and left like it's a carnival, a great party celebrating growth, prosperity, and the American way, whatever it was or hopefully would become. They would talk turkey at these meetings in the morning and then head out onto the links and make deals in the afternoon.

The Coachella Valley is all about golf. There is an enormous amount of golf played here on every level, fifteen championship courses with more on the way. They've now expanded, bringing in tennis as a second sport—but in the end, out here it will always be the golf.

At La Quinta, there is the sense of being in a Mexican hacienda, the adobe houses clustered like a small village, the Santa Rosa Mountains looming in the background. There is a hardness to this desert, it's not the soft sand of beaches; it's lunar, cold, unyielding. In the distances are desert grasses, mesquite trees, sagebrush, and under my feet the lushest, most surrealistically perfect Kodacolor-hued green grass I've ever seen.

Palm Springs and the surrounding towns are odd places, the creative life of the valley feels Stepford-like, mute, dangerous in a whole other way. Do they just play golf forever? You can't help but tune out the rest of the world, can't help but slow down and get into the rhythm of the place. However, in a moment of panic, in my need not to be muted, I hijacked a golf cart and took it for a long ride at dusk. Over the green, over the mounds, around the edges of the sand traps, riding curving hills of the golf course—it was fantastic. In the distance were men finishing their games, swinging long and hard. I watched the balls disappearing into the sky, my eye adjusting like the shutter of a camera searching to find it against the darkness. I felt like a ranger in an African game park—as a roadrunner zipped by, like a kid on an amusement park ride, the hills and mountains at the edge of the course, like papier-mâché decorations, movie-set boulders. I am a hunter, tracking the small white golf balls as they fly through the air, with none of the grace of a bird, like Mario Andretti tooling along at ten miles an hour, taking the turns with a certain devil-may-care glee. I drive around until the last of the golfers have gone home, until it is dark, until they are summoning me back, with two orange flashlights, the kind you use to direct an airplane to the gate. I feel like a cowboy. The cart is my horse, I am riding the Wild, Wild West.

When the rain stops I drive to Joshua Tree. It is hauntingly beautiful, there is snow on the ground even though the air is warm. One has the sense that magical things happen here. If you were from another planet this would be a good place to land. The surrounding community is very rough-hewn, every man for himself. There is an extreme flatness to the desert—midday there are no shadows, it is like movie lighting, like a correction that bleaches everything out, that encourages the eye to go beyond seeing, beyond the full light of day into a kind of blindness, acceptance.

There are two images of Palm Springs and Rancho Mirage that will always be with me, the first a 1961 photograph of retired President Dwight D. Eisenhower barbecuing in La Quinta, the second a 1979 photograph by Joel Sternfeld, "After a Flash Flood, Rancho Mirage, California." The image is of a sinkhole, a cave in the Earth having given way at the edge of a house. You can see the pavement and where the ground has fractured, split, fallen away, revealing striations of the Earth. A car lies upside down at the bottom of the pit. There are also broken pipes, and the sense that more of what is above ground, the house, garage, the palm trees, could give way at any minute.

In Rancho Mirage, the streets are named after former Presidents and celebrities, Gerald Ford and Bob Hope Drives. The Annenbergs' property is defined by a long pink wall, confining the greenest grass I've ever seen; the combination of the pink wall and the green grass vibrates more intensely than a

Mark Rothko painting, perhaps as intensely as a Lily Pulitzer dress. Bob Hope's house, designed in 1972 by John Lautner, looms over the edge of a cliff, visible from Highway 111. It is like a spaceship or half-deflated football, but there's no way to get a closer look—the road up is gated. In fact, all of the residential communities in the valley are gated. Given that no one is here, I'm not actually sure what they're locking in or who they are keeping out. Even the trailer parks are gated. Locals say they used to see Bob Hope in the grocery store really late at night, pushing a cart up and down the aisles. The Betty Ford Center is also in Rancho Mirage and seems like a perfect place to dry out—it is about as low-stress as it gets while maintaining a pulse. Oddly there are an enormous number of dialysis centers—interesting because dialysis is about water, about the ability to make water, to keep the system clean. All over the town there are dialysis centers and patches of bright grass. Despite the fact that this is a desert there seems to be no shortage of water. And here, unlike in Los Angeles, there are old people. They step out of the darkness of their condo units, of their trailers, their low-rise apartments into the broad shadowless daylight like living fossils, like something from *The Night of the Living Dead.* The town is filled with them, exiled Angelenos who long ago crossed the Hollywood age limit of forty and came out here to gently roam. They are leathery and heat seeking, desperate to stay warm, to stay hot, until finally they combust and turn into small heaps of ash.

I am in the desert for two days and my panic, my need for stimulation, continues to grow. I am discovering that I am a city person, I am a person starved for social interaction. I have run away in error. I call the Chateau Marmont and beg to come home. I tell them I will never do it again—it was a mistake even thinking I could leave, if only for a day or two. I feel like Dorothy in *The Wizard of Oz,* clicking my heels together— "There's no place like home." When I get back to L.A. my old room is taken, they have to put me in another room for a couple of days—the bellman is laughing as he hands over the key. I have been given an enormous suite, with a full-size dining room, a kitchen, a living room that could host fifty, and wrap-around terraces that overlook what used to be the Marlboro Man. What used to be the smoke from the Marlboro Man's cigarette is now the foam out of the top of a beer bottle; every few minutes it goes off.

I am so relieved to be home, I unpack. I put my clothing in the drawers, my toiletries in the bathroom cabinet. I think I'll stay a while.

CHAPTER EIGHT

California Dreaming

There is a Los Angeles of my childhood, of my fantasies. It is a small town where everyone is famous, where everyone knows each other—they're all friends. It is classically suburban, the houses look slightly more ornate than something seen in *Mr. Blandings Builds His Dream House.* It's the kind of place where Lucille Ball invites Doris Day over for dinner and Doris Day brings Kirk Douglas and someone goes strolling down the sidewalks of Beverly Hills carrying a tuna noodle casserole in a Pyrex dish. The men wear suits and ties, the women wear hats and gloves. There are no race problems, no poverty, everything is rich and green. Life is perfect. There is always a party and you're always invited—everyone loves everyone. It never happened. Or it did happen and it's a movie called *The Truman Show?*

The Los Angeles of my childhood is about images passed on through magazines, movie magazines, gossip magazines,

Rona Barrett's Hollywood. Barrett was the blonde doyenne of the single scoop, the sequel to Louella Parsons and Hedda Hopper, a one-woman industry turning out a stream of magazines. As an entertainment reporter, she used to do short spots from Hollywood. I still remember the distinctly New York, knowing smirk of her voice. She is now retired and recently launched a line of lavender products from her ranch in Santa Barbara.

Los Angeles was star maps, Ray-Ban glasses, convertibles, surfer boys and girls. It was pictures, lots of pictures, stars being immortalized on the Hollywood Walk of Fame, a tourist attraction started by the local Chamber of Commerce in 1961. I remember seeing movie stars down on their knees, crouched on the terrazzo of the walkway, bent as low as they could go in order to get their face and their star in the same frame.

It was a place where dreams came true, where heads of studios were big men who barked orders into the telephone, where directors dressed in cardigans to go on the set and assistants called out the magic words—"quiet on the set, rolling, action, and cut." It was a place where rough men smoked cigars, called women "broads" and threw their money around. And any which way, it was always romantic, it was always vibrant and interesting. The movie stars were clean-cut; later the standard loosened up a bit, but still remained glamorous and certainly no movie stars advertised the unshaved, unmade-bed look that rules today.

It was about Hollywood, old Hollywood, a Hollywood that for the most part was already long gone by the time I was first tuning in. The classic restaurant the Brown Derby on Vine Street survived until 1980—it's now a parking lot. Ciro's, the infamous nightclub, is now the Comedy Store. The Schwab's

Drugstore on the corner of Crescent Heights and Sunset Boulevard, frequently falsely identified as the place where Lana Turner was discovered though it is the place where Harold Arlen sat at the counter and wrote "Somewhere Over the Rainbow," is now a Virgin Megastore. Across the street and down the block from the Hollywood Walk of Fame is Fredrick's of Hollywood, the trashy lingerie store that boasts a lingerie museum. If you can allow yourself to get into a little low-level sleaze, it's quite amusing. There's Musso and Frank Grill, among the oldest of restaurants, a place where actors and writers used to hang out, among them Nathanael West, author of the classic Hollywood novel *The Day of the Locust*.

In the Hollywood of my childhood, there was no drug addiction, no alcoholism, no plastic surgery gone wrong. Everything was youth and beauty, high hopes and pearly white smiles. It was not a city tinged with thousands of tragic deaths, suicides, murders, "accidents." It had none of the shallow, over-inflated, self-centered culture of users and abusers. It wasn't a town where no one says no to your face, a town where it is hard to be alone and even worse to be lonely.

In a town obsessed with youth, a culture where twenties are prime, thirties are starting to lose their luster, forties are practically over the hill, and fifties are positively geriatric, I wondered what it was like to actually be old. It occurred to me that I'd never seen any old people in Los Angeles, not on the streets, not in restaurants, not shopping, not even shrunken down and hovering over the edge of the steering wheel, tooling down Sunset a little light on the gas.

With the exception of a few lizardy old ladies discreetly tucked into the booths of the Hotel Bel Air at lunch time— faces tight as a drum, hands now gnarly claws—it is as if old people are banned from the city of Los Angeles.

So I went looking for them. I found depressing two-story "retirement homes" showing no signs of life mixed in among commercial enterprises on very busy streets. I saw community-based senior citizen centers offering discount $1.50 lunches populated by a few downtrodden men who'd long ago lost their dentures.

At best, if you're an ancient celebrity, they trot you out for special occasions, but even that is done with great caution and at arm's length.

Hollywood celebrates immortality, the preservation of youth, the buying and selling of wrinkle-free icons. The phrase "senior citizen" connotes someone who has lived here for more than five years—it's a death-denying culture.

It's got to be hard to age in a city panicked by history, by anything with too long of a back story, by antiquity, by cracks in the surface—the city itself is all about surface: smooth, unblemished.

Face-lifts, ass-lifts, tummy tucks—in Los Angeles a body is remade on a regular basis; people go in for a little work the way folks in other cities might take the car in for an oil change. Angelenos are forever on crazy antiaging diets, injecting themselves with all kinds of vitamins, Botox, collagen, lasering themselves back to their prime, transplanting their hair, ingesting potions. There are doctors harvesting fat from people's rear ends and injecting it into their faces, anything not to look old, or better yet not to even look one's age.

Among seniors there is an enormous invisibility factor. Until he fell and broke his hip a couple of years ago, former President Reagan was reportedly often taken for walks along the Venice Beach Boardwalk—no one noticed.

The very nature of human existence in Hollywood compounds the problem. It's not a city of casual friendships, of easy access to resources. You don't see people going out for a little fresh air—no one walks around the neighborhood, except the cleaning ladies to and from the bus stop. Think about what it means to get older, to have a limited income, to not be as physically able, to live in a city with poor public transportation. There is a subway in Los Angeles, but it is a joke; more than ninety percent of people I asked didn't know about it—"You mean the monorail at Disneyland, right?" Los Angeles is an isolating place for anyone, but all the more so for seniors who can't drive.

When thinking about Los Angeles, I kept thinking I'd write about the obsession with age and gravity-defying treatments and perhaps spend some time in a plastic surgeon's office, but then it occurred to me that I really wanted to find the old folks and more specifically, the old folks of Hollywood. I remembered that every year on the Academy Awards they make mention of the Motion Picture and Television Fund Retirement Community, which used to be known as the Old Actors' Home. I found that the fund dates back to 1921, when Hollywood was still a small pioneer town and the organization was known as the Motion Picture Relief Fund, the idea behind it being that the motion picture community needed to take care of its own. Originally headed up by top stars like Mary Pickford, the fund raised money to be distributed on a "relief first, questions second" basis to cover emergency expenses such as rent, medical assistance, funerals, and help people find work, etc. Contributions to the fund became a payroll deduction in 1931 equal to a half percent of earnings. Many of those who came to Hollywood in the early days left behind families in the East and Midwest and either never married or had marriages that failed. This left them all the more on their own and socially and financially dependent upon the Hollywood community.

The main campus of the retirement village is located on a forty-eight-acre spread in Woodland Hills, and at this point is part of an extended health-care network serving the entire motion picture and entertainment industry—from children to seniors. The retirement facilities include independent and assisted living. The Country House, with its Jeanette McDonald Dining Room and Douglas Fairbanks Lounge, is for those who are able to manage on their own, as is the new Fran and Ray Stark Villa. On the grounds there is the Wasserman Koi Pond, the Roddy McDowall Rose Garden, exercise facilities in the Katzenberg Pavilions and church services in the John Ford Chapel. The Frances Goldwyn Lodge is an assisted-living facility and there's also Harry's Haven, an Alzheimer's unit, given by Kirk and Anne Douglas and named in honor of Kirk's father.

One thinks of retirement homes as halfway houses between living and dying. It is a difficult decision for the retiree and his or her family to move into such a facility. We are people who pride ourselves on independence, and while aging may seem to be a universal issue, it's in many ways a very American issue, reflecting the structure of the society and the family, disparate, fractured. We don't think of the elderly as the wise, the leisured, nor do we acknowledge the importance of the history they hold, their role in the life cycle, their ability to be role models for the next generation.

My visual fantasy/nightmare of the actors home was rolling farmland where aged actors and actresses roamed in costumes reflecting their heyday, cowboys in western wear, frontier ladies in bustle skirts, a few hepcats from the 1950s with painted-on hair, all of them put out to pasture like retired racehorses. In reality, it initially appears to be much like any other retirement community, a series of low buildings built and expanded over the years. But what's significantly different about this facility is the sense of community. And the heat—there is an other-worldly quality to the heat, the baking sun. If you've ever noticed, old people have a hard time regulating their tempera-ture—they're always cold, always needing a sweater—but not here. It's a kind of nirvana in shirt sleeves.

Everyone here has something in common—the industry—whether as prop men, costumers, camera operators, actors and actresses; theirs is a shared experience. There are frequent screenings of new releases in their movie theater and guest visits by industry heavyweights. And at a time in one's life when long-term memory functions better than short, when the impetus to make new connections is dwindling and where there is com-fort to be had in the past, folks here are happy to swap stories of the way it used to be and, equally important, continue to feel that they are part of the active community.

I met for tea with four residents, Virginia McDowall, the sister of Roddy McDowall, who curiously enough had been at the 1941 groundbreaking of the facility shortly after she and Roddy had arrived in California. In her droll English accent, Virginia shared her magnificent story of coming to America by boat.

Hal Riddle, a character actor who has a schoolboy's enthusiasm, radiated the thrill of having lucked into something great. A movie fan since he was a boy, he used to write away for autographed pictures from his childhood home in Kentucky. We were joined in the dining room by Tommy Farrell and his wife Bobbi—Tommy is the son of movie star Glenda Farrell and essentially grew up on movie sets, having had a significant career of his own as an actor, in films, television, night clubs, vaudeville—you name it, Tommy did it.

I had hoped to talk with them about growing old—interestingly the subject never came up. We talked about everything else—their careers, who they worked with, how they made their way to Hollywood, what the scene used to be like. The fact that the subject of age never became part of the conversation meant to me that they don't think of themselves as old, they think of themselves first and foremost as actors and they weren't going to let me forget it.

MS. HOMES: So tell me your names again.

MR. FARRELL: Tommy. And this is Bobbi, B-O-B-B-I, Farrell. F as in Frank, A-R-R-E-L-L.

MS. HOMES: And where were you born?

MR. FARRELL: In Hollywood. My mother was Glenda Farrell, and she was a big star at Warner Brothers.

I grew up on the Warner Brothers lot. So I thought, gee, this is the only business to be in. [laughter] After school every day, we had a chauffeur and houseman, and he would pick me up at school, and then we drove to the studio and waited for mom to be finished. ... I got to know a lot of people. Jimmy Cagney, and Bogart, and all the Warner brothers sons.

MRS. FARRELL: But you stayed out here when your mother first went back to Broadway, right?

MR. FARRELL: No that was in '39 where she went back to New York. I went to St. John's Military Academy.

MS. HOMES: Did you ever think you might go into the military?

MR. FARRELL: No. I thought I might be a cowboy for a while, and I was. I went to the University of Arizona, and in the spring and fall roundups, they would hire kids from school. I played polo there for two years. And my grandpa was an old horse trader. So he told me how to handle the rope when I was about six or so. I roped every cat and dog in the neighborhood! [laughter]

MS. HOMES: And when you worked as a cowboy, were you the only kid from Hollywood working as a cowboy?

MR. FARRELL: Yes.

MS. HOMES: And did you really rope?

MR. FARRELL: Yes, I did. I roped right up until 1992 ... '93 ... I used to do the Ben Johnson Pro-Celebrity.

MRS. FARRELL: There weren't many cowboys in cowboy pictures. He never knew which he wanted to be, a cowboy or an actor.

MR. FARRELL: I really wanted to be a cowboy, but acting paid better.

MS. HOMES: Funny how that is!

MR. FARRELL: But I guess you could say I was pretty much of a rounded actor. I started out on Broadway, did three shows, then I went into nightclubs and vaudeville. I went into television—movies first, and then television. I was under contract to Desilu; I did a series there. I did eleven shows with Lucy, and twenty-two shows with Red Skelton. And I headlined in Vegas. I headlined the Palace in New York in vaudeville, in 1953. Opened the Fontainebleau down in Miami. I played Ciro's here.

MS. HOMES: And how did you two meet?

MR. FARRELL: Blind date.

MRS. FARRELL: We've been married forty years.

MR. FARRELL: Yeah. We went out to dinner at a place called Steer's Restaurant, on La Cienega.

MS. HOMES: And how did it go?

MR. FARRELL: She thought I was crazy!

MS. HOMES: Hal, how long have you guys known each other?

MR. RIDDLE: When I was a youngster, I used to read about him with his mother, and I'd see his picture in the magazines, so when I came here you can imagine what a surprise ... you know, as a kid I used to see his picture, and we talked about Glenda Farrell, with her little boy. Little Tommy. And he'd be with her because they were really inseparable.

MR. FARRELL: I was in a show in New York, and he came to see it.

MR. RIDDLE: *Barefoot Boy with Cheek.* That was the name of it. And it starred Nancy Walker.

MR. FARRELL: And Red Buttons.

MR. RIDDLE: And written by Max Shulman, who wrote an awful lot of good stuff. But I remember it was in 1946, that was on Broadway.

MRS. FARRELL: Isn't that the one you got immediately after the war?

MR. FARRELL: Yeah. I got out of the army. I was in the Army Air Force. We did this show on Broadway, and then we went to Europe, and we were a five-man unit. We used to do hospitals, you know? Entertain the guys in the hospital, in the wards. Red Buttons was one of the guys. He taught me how to dance and we did a dance act. ... I got out of the army, and two weeks later I was in the play.

MR. RIDDLE: I didn't become a professional actor until I was twenty-eight. I went into summer stock, my roommate was Jack Lemmon. My first summer stock was 1948, at Hayloft Summer theater. And Jack was the resident juvenile. And I played small parts, and was a secretary to the director and the producer. Then when Jack finished his plays there that summer, he didn't finish, he left three plays before it ended. He went to New York to do his first TV show, called *That Wonderful Guy.* And then I took over his roles in the summer theater. And we've been friends ever since.

MS. HOMES: Where were you born?

MR. RIDDLE: Calhoun, Kentucky. Green River in Kentucky.

MS. HOMES: When did you come to California?

MR. RIDDLE: I was in New York City doing stage work for twelve years, from '48 to '57. I did my first film in New York City, called *Cop Hater*, with Robert Loggia. And then I was called out here in 1957 to do *Onionhead* at Warner Brothers with Andy Griffith. And I've been here ever since.

MS. HOMES: When you moved out here, where did you move to?

MR. RIDDLE: Hmm, it's very interesting. Because when New York actors get out here, the first thing they tell you is the Chateau Marmont. Well, I call the Chateau Marmont and they said uh, we're absolutely booked, we're not supposed to tell you this, but the New York actors we can't handle go to the Montecito in Hollywood. So boy, I barreled right to the Montecito. But when you read movie magazines, boy you knew about the Chateau Marmont. Garbo stayed there! And some of the great stars. Jean Harlow, in between one or two of her marriages, she went there. I lived in Santa Monica before I got out here. And I loved it very much. Of course I really like it here. Boy, for retirement this is the ideal place.

MR. FARRELL: Nothing can touch this place.

MRS. FARRELL: Nothing.

MR. FARRELL: In the whole country, or Europe. Nothing is that good.

MRS. FARRELL: They hide it. It's a hideaway. When he first got cancer, they put him on the list.

MR. RIDDLE: They used to call this the best kept secret in the industry.

MRS. FARRELL: A. M., I'd like to introduce you to ... Virginia, let me introduce you to A. M.

MS. HOMES: Virginia, were you born here? In California?

MS. MCDOWALL: No, London. We arrived in New York on October 3, 1940.

MS. HOMES: And when did you come to California?

MS. MCDOWALL: Almost immediately. We both did the test for *How Green Was My Valley.* And they put him under contract right away—we hardly had a moment. They whisked us to the Beverly Wilshire.

MR. RIDDLE: Now, I decided when I was about nine years old that I was gonna come to Hollywood. And I lived in Dawson Springs, Kentucky. It's funny how we had different paths. ... My idea was to come here and be a movie star.

MS. HOMES: And Tommy, when you were a kid and your mom was a big movie star, did it occur to you, "Oh my mom is a big movie star?" Or you just thought, this is my life.

MR. FARRELL: That's where she works—at Warner Brothers. That was her job. And she worked hard, and I realized that was no picnic either. Especially being under contract at Warner's at the time, she would do two and three pictures at the same time. And run from one stage, change costumes, and on the other stage. Change, then go back to the other stage.

MRS. FARRELL: That was one of the problems of contracts. They have a contract with you and they just throw you everywhere.

MR. RIDDLE: And they just use them like they do racehorses.

MR. FARRELL: I was fifteen years old before I found out that that-son-of-a-bitch-Jack-Gordon wasn't one word! [laughter]

MS. HOMES: Virginia, what are some of your earliest memories of working in the industry?

MS. MCDOWALL: I acted a little bit in *Man Hunt,* as the postmistress's daughter. With Tyrone Power and Joan Fontaine, of course. That was the first. Apropos of nothing, but drinking tea, I was talking to someone the other day ... this has nothing to do with anything, but I have a theory about how England won the war! [laughter]

MRS. FARRELL: With tea?

MS. MCDOWALL: With tea! Because after every bombing, you know, you'd come up out of the cellar, or wherever, whatever hole, and someone would say, put the kettle on, let's have a cup of tea! And everyone carried a thermos and a gas mask. [laughter]

MS. HOMES: What is it like to be in a community here where everyone did work in the industry? It's obviously very different from being in any other retirement place where you arrive and no one knows who you are.

MRS. FARRELL: It really is the commonality that makes it a community.

MR. RIDDLE: I think what makes it kind of unique also, and you've heard me mention this before—other people, when they retire, they leave the people they work with, and they're put out to pasture. They're given the gold watch or whatever, and then they're through. We retire here, and then we move out here, and we go right on being a part of our industry. We stopped acting in front of the camera or doing whatever we did behind, but now we're still part of the family. We go right on. Which is really quite a remarkable thing when you stop to think about it.

MS. MCDOWALL: My brother and I used to entertain out here in the 40s when we were kids.

MS. HOMES: Virginia, how did it happen that you were here for the ground breaking?

MS. MCDOWALL: Well, because we had arrived in October, as I said. And Rod, it was a great year of publicity about him prior to the movie, And I guess someone invited him. [laughter]

MRS. FARRELL: His PR man. [laughter]

MS. HOMES: Virginia, how long have you lived here?

MS. MCDOWALL: Nine years.

MS. HOMES: And where were you living before you moved here?

MS. MCDOWALL: I was living in Hollywood.

MR. RIDDLE: Well you came at a very interesting time, because it was right in the middle of the war. I mean we hadn't gotten into it. It was the middle of your war, just before we got into it. You came in '40.

MS. MCDOWALL: Yeah, we used to spend time at the Hollywood Canteen. Rod was a busboy, and my mother ran the Coca-Cola stand. It was a different time, too. They wouldn't let me dance, because I was too young. I think my big memory of nightclubs was when we got all dressed up and my brother took me to see Edith Piaf. And I cried my heart out. I've never forgotten that.

MR. RIDDLE: That reminds me of when I went to see Judy at the Palace. Oh, I tell you. It was just one of those performances you'll never forget.

MRS. FARRELL: Tommy dated Judy.

MR. RIDDLE: Yes he did.

MR. FARRELL: Judy was my prom date!

MS. HOMES: Notice how you guys say Judy. Now in my generation we say Julia.

MR. FARRELL: But she was my prom date, my senior prom. We went in an MGM big limousine! With an MGM chauffeur.

MRS. FARRELL: How old was she?

MR. FARRELL: Judy was fifteen.

MRS. FARRELL: And you were?

MR. FARRELL: Sixteen. I met Judy at the Jitterbug House, with Sid Miller, and Jackie. And we hit it off, and she liked to dance, and I was a jitterbugging devil! [laughter]

MR. RIDDLE: Oh I tell you. Jitterbugging was our era.

MRS. FARRELL: Everyone wanted to be a drummer then.

MS. HOMES: Virginia, did you want to be a drummer? [laughter]

MS. MCDOWALL: No darling. I wanted to be a stage actress. I wanted to be Ellen Terry and marry Errol Flynn.

MR. RIDDLE: You know, most little boys have Babe Ruth for their hero. I had Clark Gable. He was the one, he was the big hero ... if you ever see my cottage, I've got Gable pictures all over. Autographs. And of course my big dream was to be in a picture with Clark Gable. Well, as it turned out, I came to Hollywood, and I hadn't been out here very long, and I needed a haircut, and a friend of mine says, "I belong to the Bel Air Country Club. Come out and use our barber." He said, "It's for members only, but by all means use him, he's so good." So I came out there, and I was having my hair cut, and I was always very sensitive about my big ears. And I told him, "Now don't cut too much around ..." And he said, "Well, it never bothered Clark Gable." And I said, "Why? Did you cut his hair?" He said, "Well, I cut his hair." And so we got to talking. I said, "Do you think some day when you know Gable is coming ...?" And sure enough, he set it up and I got to meet him and talk to him.

MS. HOMES: For all of you, coming here from another country, growing up here—can you talk a little bit about both the fantasy of Hollywood and the dream? You lived the dream.

MS. MCDOWALL: Well, we fell into it because of the war. That's it, to get away from the war.

MR. RIDDLE: My big dream had been built up by

going to movies and reading the fan magazines. And just the glory of it, I got to do all this in the golden era. We had a Warner Brothers theater in my little town. I saw all the Warner Brothers pictures, MGM, all the big ones. So you see, I had a dream of Hollywood, and had I been able to come out here, as a teenager ... it would have been so great. But by the time I got out here in '57, the bubble had burst. The studios were breaking up. All the contract lists were going. I went to Warner Brothers to do my first picture. Imagine! Warner Brothers, where the gods lived on Olympus. And I went into the commissary and there was no one there. There were only two other pictures filming on the whole lot! *Marjorie Morning Star,* and the ending of *The Old Man and the Sea.*

MS. HOMES: Tommy, do you feel like there was a moment where it did start to fall apart?

MR. FARRELL: Well, the government decided that if you were a studio you shouldn't own your own theaters anymore. And Warner Brothers, MGM, Paramount, they all got rid of their own theaters. Up to that point, every studio had an actors school, and they trained them. They taught them how to sing and dance, and ride horseback, and fence, and whatever the hell, you know. And the studios broke up.

MS. HOMES: Right. Virginia, you were in England and because of the war things were getting bad in England? How did you end up coming to the United States?

MS. MCDOWALL: We were there during the first

spring year of the war, and we were not evacuated. We stayed in London, so I experienced a lot of the bombings. And my brother collected shrapnel like crazy. [laughter] All little boys did. And I sat there being petrified. Then the ship was ready—we went to Liverpool and were bombed like crazy. They were bombing Liverpool, because it was a port.

MS. HOMES: How old were you and your brother?

MS. MCDOWALL: I had my thirteenth birthday on the ship. My brother was twelve, going on twelve.

MS. HOMES: And your dad just sent the two of you on your own?

MS. MCDOWALL: No, no, with mother, who couldn't wait to get to Hollywood. It was the best thing that ever happened to her! My mother was a rather volcanic lady. She was really an enormously interesting person, and a great raconteur. She had a gorgeous operatic voice; she had sung with Sousa in Fairmount Park in Philadelphia. I think her mother had wanted to be an actress. So it was a vicarious dream for her. Because we did work in England. My brother did sixteen films, and I think I did eight. So that when we did come in to New York, we had done a scene at the ship's party. We did "Puck and the Fairy" from *A Midsummer Night's Dream.* My mother just happened to have the costumes! [laughter] In the trunk, in this tiny cabin.

MR. FARRELL: Of course!

MR. RIDDLE: Not that she was a stage mother at all. No. Uh uh.

MS. MCDOWALL: She was really too much. So anyway, we did "Puck and the Fairy," and then the ship docked. And people would say "Oh you should see those two darling little children!" [laughter] And they took photographs. There was a photograph in the *New York Times*. And some enterprising young man, either at Fox or the William Morris Agency, looked us up in the ... they called it the *Spotlight* in England, a player's directory. And that's when Fox called and did the test.

MS. HOMES: You didn't even know that was going to happen?

MS. MCDOWALL: No, we were supposed to live in White Plains, New York.

MS. HOMES: How glamorous was Hollywood when you got here?

MS. MCDOWALL: Well you must remember, we were children, in a sense. Although we did go to a lot of premieres, and stuff like that. The studio did a lot of publicity. Well, of course everyone was very glamorous.

MS. HOMES: Tommy, was your life very glamorous as a child, would you say?

MR. FARRELL: Oh yeah! We had parties at the house. And my mother was dating Cary Grant. No, my mother was dating his roommate, Randolph Scott. And Mary Ryan was my mother's best friend, and she was dating Cary Grant. And they would come over to the house. And one day ... I shouldn't tell it. Yeah, I can tell it. [laughter] Louella Parsons. And her husband, Doc Martin.

MRS. FARRELL: Harry. Was it Harry?

MR. RIDDLE: It was Harry.

MR. FARRELL: Harry Martin.

MR. RIDDLE: Doc, they called him.

MR. FARRELL: Doc. And he drank a little bit.

MR. RIDDLE: Yes.

MR. FARRELL: Well so did she. At the house in Studio City, the living room was very French, pastel. And we had a big Louis XV couch in pastel blue satin. And, after about four or five martinis, Louella is sitting there on the couch, and she had an accident.

MR. RIDDLE: Oh my God!

MRS. FARRELL: Oh no!

MR. RIDDLE: And I said, Mom! Whup. [laughter]

MR. FARRELL: I was gonna say Lally just peed on the couch! [laughter]

MR. RIDDLE: Lally peed on the couch! [claps hands] I love it. I didn't read those in the movie magazines.

CHAPTER NINE

The Castle on the Hill

"One story that I always loved," says Griffin Dunne, *"a friend of mine brought her best girlfriend out to see her. The girlfriend was from a little working class town in Massachusetts ... a real wild party girl. I always pictured sort of Joan Cusack in* Working Girl. *Big hair, and big-boned, and really wild. So they went to a Hollywood party, and she met her favorite movie star. And all of a sudden ... the girl was gone. She went off with the movie star. And they didn't see her all night, but she got a call—'I'm in his house. It's the biggest house you ever saw.' And she goes 'Well, where is it?' 'I don't know. But I'll call you tomorrow and I'll figure it out. I'm going to stay here. You wouldn't believe the hallways. It's like a big French castle—it's this enormous house, and the kitchen is so small.' So the next morning this girl finds out that her girlfriend was staying at the Chateau. The guy had told her that it was his house!"*

More than anything, the Chateau Marmont reminds me of one of the most sacred places in my own life—Yaddo, an artists' colony, a magical castle, hidden in the woods among the tall northern pines near Saratoga Springs, New York. As there are those who believe the Chateau Marmont is built upon a kind of energy vortex, a creative meridian, there are people who strongly believe that the land Yaddo rests on is a source of great power. At both Yaddo and the Chateau, I am able to get more work done in several weeks than I can in months at home. My powers of concentration are enhanced, as is my imagination. In the 1830s and 1840s, a popular tavern operated by Jacobus Barhyte stood on the site where Yaddo is now. Numerous well-known writers of the period dined at the tavern—it is believed that Edgar Allan Poe wrote part of *The Raven* on that land.

Like the Chateau, each of Yaddo's rooms are different and you never know exactly where you will be until you arrive. There is the same cool dark cave-like interior, heavy velvet draperies, deep old sofas covered in crushed velvet, large carved chairs, and stained-glass windows. The only difference between Yaddo and the Chateau is that the Chateau is a hotel open to anyone who makes a reservation and pays the room charges. One must apply to Yaddo, submit samples of work and ultimately be chosen to come—at Yaddo one is truly a guest. The Chateau Marmont is, in effect, an artistic enclave, "frayed around the edges with a touch of the old Hollywood glamour. It is a place where a lot of different worlds come together, a hub for the creative community," says Lisa Phillips, director of New York's New Museum for Contemporary Art.

"I'll tell you another thing," John Waters says. "The only time I didn't stay at the Chateau when I came to L.A., I did not get my movie deal. So I'm really superstitious. I stayed at that one down on the corner on the other side? Where a lot of rock and roll people stay. I didn't get the movie deal and I got the flu."

Hotels are the stuff of stories, mini-dramas. An entire world operates behind the scenes, making the running of the hotel seem effortless. The staff itself is a community not unlike a small town, not unlike something you'd find in Sherwood Anderson's *Winesburg, Ohio,* or Thornton Wilder's *Our Town,* not unlike a postmodern *Peyton Place,* or an American version of *Fawlty Towers.* Among the staff of reservation agents, housekeepers, kitchen workers, prep cooks, waiters and waitresses, car jockeys, managers, engineers, pages, the night auditor, are those who have been working at the Chateau for ten to twenty years or more. And what becomes apparent when talking with people who have been staying at the Chateau year after year, is that the staff is as much identified with the place as anything— numerous people spoke with me about the man who used to answer the phone in the 1970s.

"I always thought it might be interesting to find the guy who answered the phone," Griffin Dunne confessed one day. "You know who I mean? He was as famous as the Moviefone guy is now."

"The most fantastic thing was the guy behind the front desk who would answer the phone, {deep voice} 'Chateau.' He was amazing," Jennifer Beals also remembered. "You would sometimes just

want to call the hotel just to hear him say 'Chateau.' It was like performance art. He was like an European aristocrat—he would tolerate you, but let you know that you were calling a place that was very wealthy, and old, and weren't you lucky to be calling! And yet it was not a put-off, it was incredibly charming. I would love to know what that guy's name is."

Pat Abedi is the current hotel operator. She mans the switchboard in the back office, a small cramped area just behind the front desk. This area is command central for the entire hotel; nothing happens that the folks sitting here don't know about first. To sit with Pat is to have the consummate backstage pass, to be an absolute insider, and it's an incredibly good time.

"Good morning, Chateau Marmont, one moment I'll connect you." "Good morning, Chateau Marmont, I'm sorry there's no one here by that name." "Chateau Marmont, can you hold?" The phone rings as many as twenty times in a minute and she remains incredibly down to earth, focused, unflappable. She has been answering hotel phones for years. She is sometimes funny, sometimes makes faces at annoying callers, sometimes uses a foreign accent. Pat is like the reference librarian for the hotel. There is a bulletin board in the back office with special instructions—"BE CAREFUL, THERE ARE TWO SMITHS IN HOUSE"—like a hospital where you wouldn't want to mix food trays or medications. Another sign says MR.____ IS A VERY IMPORTANT VIP, PLEASE BE CAREFUL WITH HIS MESSAGES AND MAIL. There are also signs giving the code names for various super-famous guests. I have no idea how often these names change and who makes them up, I also have the impression that it's best not to ask, best to pretend not to have noticed in the first place. An enormous amount of information passes though the switchboard, much of it from nameless voices. Does Pat care if she's talking to a famous person?—truly not. One complication of fame is that it can bring with it a peculiar kind of entitlement, the expectation that things should happen more easily, more quickly, simply because a person is recognizable. When I ask Pat about what it's like to deal with famous people all the time, she is genuinely not interested. She likes the guests who are nice to her, and can't be bothered with those who cop an attitude.

Across from Pat sits Carol O'Brien, currently the director of Human Resources. If you want a job at the Chateau, she's the one you have to talk to. Carol has worked at the hotel for twelve years and has seen it through a variety of incarnations. She lives just about an hour from Sunset Boulevard on a farm with two horses, a dog, China, two cats, Bill and Dorothy, chickens and rabbits, and homegrown vegetables among other things. She used to have two iguanas, Hector and Liz, but their relationship became abusive, with Hector beating up Liz, and so Hector was sent on his way. She tells me a story about a longtime hotel guest, a man who had been both an illustrator and a famed pearl diver who divided his time between the Chateau Marmont and Cabo, Mexico. He had several dogs, one of which had a litter of puppies in his room at the Chateau—the pups were dubbed the Chateau Mar-mutts. He called Carol from Cabo after finding out that he was ill and asked if she might come down to pick him up and bring him back to the Chateau. And it wasn't just that he needed a ride—he had the dogs and all his worldly goods with him. After agreeing to meet at a place somewhere between Cabo and Hollywood, Carol and a friend set off in a truck and rescued the fellow and brought him back to the hotel, where he passed away soon after. And while Carol seemed to think that this wasn't a particularly good story because it didn't have the happiest of endings, it struck me as a perfect illustration of not only the profound attachment of the staff to the guests, but also the notion that someone terminally ill would want to return to the hotel, the place he identified as home.

Erin Foti, design director of the hotel, is responsible for the subtle changes, the things you wouldn't exactly notice on their own. The cumulative effect has been a wonderful reconsideration, a slow upgrading of the hotel's spaces, furnishings, design aesthetic. She is involved with everything—the color of the wicker chairs under the colonnade, the fabrics on the sofa, the paintings in the lobby living room, the plantings one sees in the garden areas. Maintaining the look of the hotel is like taking care of a heavily trafficked great house; something always needs updating.

Among the longtime guests there was a strong resistance to change. Just after Andre Balazs had completed his renovation and redecoration, some of the guests would arrive and request that the old furniture be put back into their rooms. The Chateau, being the Chateau of course, had the old furniture on hand and would return it to the room, only to take it out again after the guest checked out.

"I never resisted any of the renovation," says John Waters. "I think it looks nice. In the courtyard. I always throw a penny in that

fountain. It's a goddamn wishing well. Right out front by the door, there's a little water there. I always throw coins there, like a fool! I never would think of doing that anywhere else in the world. {funny voice} Because I think my wishes will come true there!"

I ask Erin if she think the hotel is built upon some kind of energy field. She tells me about a recent trip she took to India for the Kumbha Mela Festival, one of India's most significant spiritual festivals, occurring once every twelve years and drawing millions of people. Part of the festival involves taking a ritual bath in the magical waters found at the confluence of three rivers: the Ganges, the Yamuna, and the Saraswati—an invisible spiritual river. Erin brought back waters from this festival, water from the Ganges, and added a little bit of it to each of the pools of water at the hotel—the fountain, the koi pool, the pond with a Buddha at one end, the swimming pool, and the wishing well that John Waters mentioned. The myth or legend being that any water that mixes with Ganges water becomes Ganges water—magic water. She also brings Nag Champa incense, which burns around the pool. It is India's most popular meditation incense and has been used for deep calming meditation and for creating sacred spaces.

"When people breathe in the incense, it changes them spiritually. They don't know this. but I personally believe it—it brings memories to people that they're not aware of, memories of ancient experience, it awakens us," she tells me as we are touring the property. The scent is inescapable; I breathe deeply.

The man who oversees the hotel is thirty-two-year-old general manager Philip Pavel. Slightly larger than life, he's six foot two and moves through the hotel with ghostlike grace, deftly handling the stickiest of situations with a homespun sense of humor.

MS. HOMES: Where did you grow up?

MR. PAVEL: I grew up in Hickory Hills, Illinois. Which is on the southwest side of Chicago. As you're coming off the I-55 expressway, the Double Nickel, as they call it in Chicago.

MS. HOMES: Why do they call it the Double Nickel?

MR. PAVEL: Because it's two fives in there, I-55. Right where the turnoff is to go to Hickory Hills, you go way out by what they call the "shit pits," where they process all of the human waste for all of the city of Chicago. So it just smells terrible. And as you pass that, you pass the Wonder bread factory, which smells wonderful! And for some reason, these two extremes, shit and Wonder bread, seem to sum up my suburban childhood to me! [laughs]

MS. HOMES: What kind of people lived there?

MR. PAVEL: Working-class. South side Chicago. You were either Polish, Italian, or Irish. Mostly white working-class ghetto.

MS. HOMES: And then how did you end up coming to California?

MR. PAVEL: I studied acting at Northwestern. I knew that I wanted to be an actor at about eight. Northwestern took pride in calling itself the Harvard of the

Midwest. A lot of the kids were really pretentious. They would say, What do you want to do when you graduate? I want to create great art. And I remember thinking that I had to rebel against all that. So I said, I'm gonna go to L.A. and I'm going to be on a sitcom. And I'm gonna sell out in a New York minute and make lots of money. ... I was known as L.A. Phil long before I ever came to L.A. And I always liked that when I first arrived in L.A., the L.A. Philharmonic had big posters all around town that said L.A. Phil. That all seemed right.

MS. HOMES: When did you come here?

MR. PAVEL: I got here right after I graduated, so in the fall of '91. The great California recession of '91! I couldn't find a job, and I was so naïve, still being from the Midwest, that I didn't lie on my résumé. But, as fate would have it, in the case of L.A. style over substance, I got cast in my first job. I applied for a job as a waiter at the Café Plaza, the coffee shop in the Century Plaza Hotel. But they needed a maître d' for their French restaurant. I was twenty-two and had no business being a maître d', had no experience, but even though I'm a hybrid of mostly Polish, German, Austrian, Russian, English, Irish, Lithuanian, they thought I looked like I could be French! My real last name is Pawelczyk, but Philip Pawelczyk became Philippe Pavel, and I was reborn. But Pawelczyk I was happy to throw out. I never looked back!

MS. HOMES: Does the rest of your family go by Pawelczyk?

MR. PAVEL: Yes ... they were very upset at first because I'm a junior. ... But my parents, now that they've seen me in a movie and stuff, they think the name's very glamorous. And sometimes when they order a pizza they'll feel a little dangerous, and they'll say Pavel instead of Pawelczyk.

MS. HOMES: And when you were thinking that you wanted to grow up and come here, what was Los Angeles to you?

MR. PAVEL: I read Bret Easton Ellis when I was in high school. And the city seemed very glamorous to me—kids who just had tons of money and did cocaine. It all seemed dangerous and decadent. I listened to a lot of Duran Duran in my bedroom in Hickory Hills. MTV had just come out ... through music videos and also through movies—Richard Gere in *American Gigolo*—L.A. was this sexy place where there was lots of neon and people wore designer jeans.

MS. HOMES: One of the things that interests me about L.A., is that it's a place where people come to find themselves.

MR. PAVEL: That whole go west young man kind of thing. I definitely, in retrospect, moved to L.A. because I was south side, working-class Chicago, and I had to move as far away from home to deal with my sexuality and come out.

When I first moved here, I had this miserable day-to-day, trying to scrape for sustenance, existence. But at night, I would wear these crazy outfits, and thought I was the whiter Lenny Kravitz. And would go to clubs and was just this big club kid—but there I was, in my fantasy life, I was in L.A., and I was going to be discovered.

MS. HOMES: And did that happen?

MR. PAVEL: Mm, no.

MS. HOMES: How long were you Philippe Pavel?

MR. PAVEL: Only for the two and a half years I was at La Chaumiere, which means "country retreat."

MS. HOMES: What other jobs did you have before you ended up at the Chateau?

MR. PAVEL: At La Chaumiere, I kind of cut my teeth in the restaurant business The Century Plaza Tower was a testament to the Reagan-era 80s. So it was sort of Miss Havisham ... a really grand environment, but its heyday was long past. We served a veal chop in morel mushroom cream sauce, and there was a silver dome, and we would literally pull it off and "voilà!" But we never had any business. So I got hired to be a maître d' at Barney Greengrass, on top of Barneys New York. And that was my first time in a very sort of "scene" type environment. We were right across the street from UTA, and down the street from CAA, and that was a total baptism by fire. I learned to deal with the entertainment industry. And I got yelled at a lot.

MS. HOMES: Really? By who?

MR. PAVEL: By agents. Agents were the worst. And everyone needed to get in and out of there ... in an hour ... but have the corner table. And I was naïve. ...

It was a real education in terms of how the social system, the class system in Los Angeles works.

MS. HOMES: How would you describe that social system?

MR. PAVEL: I guess it's knowing who has heat. People in L.A. are heat-seeking missiles. And that's the whole thing you were talking about, in terms of you're only as good as your last project. So it's a subtle ... it's being able to judge the few millimeters between the falling box-office star and the rising TV star. But I always took great pride in what I thought was Midwest integrity; that if you made a reservation, and you were nice to me at the maître d' stand, you got a better table than the TV actor who actually would yell, "I'm famous, doesn't that mean anything?" I kind of saw myself as a Robin Hood.

MS. HOMES: Did it demystify celebrity culture?

MR. PAVEL: I always thought that actors had something extra, something special. That they must have been really, really beautiful, or really, really smart. And what I realize now is that, it's only after people are movie stars that they have that thing. Because people are so gaga, because our culture so worships celebrity. They don't have that to begin with. It's all something that's in people's minds that they project.

MS. HOMES: Was L.A. a place that allowed you to become yourself in a way that you probably wouldn't have in Illinois?

MR. PAVEL: Oh. definitely. There was this decadence, this sexual freedom. And I also studied Latin in high school, six years of Latin. I equated sexual freedom with this level of decadence. L.A. seems like the modern day equivalent of Rome.

MS. HOMES: OK, so back to the story.

MR. PAVEL: The people who had hired me at Barneys, who had been fired, were living at the Chateau and they had spoken to Andre about the Chateau's evolution—they wanted to upgrade the food and beverage. I guess they had frozen pizzas, and they had a four-burner stove with a handle hanging off it. Henry and Melanie were the consultants. ... They knew I was a really hard worker, they knew I was smart, but I was also young and they could get me for a song. I had never been to the Chateau. I remember I read *Interview* magazine in high school diligently. And I remember seeing the ads, and it was always sort of this mysterious place. And I came up and I sat in one of their tan chairs out in the colonnade out there, and immediately fell in love with the place. They sang me this siren song about how it would be perfect, it's a small hotel, it's only sixty-three rooms, they have a new no-party policy, so all you have to do is run room service, and there's about five tables in the lobby. And you can come or go for auditions whenever you want. I'm sold. So I did it. That was six years ago, 1996. It was non-stop parties. One after the other.

MS. HOMES: Okay, so you got here.

MR. PAVEL: Got here and ... there was no menu. There were no recipes. So if Romulo was working and you ordered a Caesar salad, Romulo made it the way Romulo thought a Caesar salad should be made. If Mike was working, Mike made it the way Mike thought it should be made. In retrospect people always think it was so charming, it was so kooky back then, but in reality it was really bad service!

MS. HOMES: There seems to be a phenomenon where people do stay here for long periods of time.

MR. PAVEL: It just lends itself toward that because it was built as an apartment complex. People stay here for months. In the six years I've been here there have been people who've lived here for over a year.

MS. HOMES: And do they just get one big bill at the end?

MR. PAVEL: They pay it like they pay rent, on a monthly basis.

MS. HOMES: How would you describe what you do on a daily basis?

MR. PAVEL: There's a lot of boring technical stuff, the budgets and the money but the main job is to make sure that everyone's happy. In the morning you check to see who's arriving, and you decide what rooms they're going in. But before they arrive you call to see if there's anything special that they need—it's kind of like throwing a dinner party every day. And you have your list of things to do and you're rushing to make it through.

MS. HOMES: And do you have to remember all that stuff?

MR. PAVEL: I would say ninety percent of our clientele has been repeat business, people who love the hotel and come back over and over. We're in the service industry.

So your goal is to make them not want for anything while they're here. The Chateau had this quirky charm of not being corporate. I think people were drawn to it for its history, for its aesthetics. It didn't have that cookie-cutter feel of the drones with the plastic name tags, always having the same rehearsed lines. But we want to get it to a point where if we notice the guest in the room always has a certain empty box of chocolates and a certain copy of the *New Yorker,* that the next time they check in, we already have it before they even ask for it. In college I was known for giving really great parties. Part of being ostracized my entire youth was that my entire adult life has been this big make-up for being alone all through my childhood. It's my job to socialize with the guests, and get to know them. And that's been the most rewarding thing because that's what doesn't feel like work at all. I've always loved to get to know people over dinner, over good food, and over a drink. And the fact that I get paid to do that is amazing.

MS. HOMES: How has the job affected your acting aspirations?

MR. PAVEL: I still love performing. I still work a lot more than a lot of other people I know. The very nature of acting is that you have a lot of free time on your hands, especially a thirty-two-year-old openly gay male. I get three weeks vacation time a year that I never take. And if I get a guest star on a TV show I take a week off and it feels like vacation. We did a television show, and the other actors on the set had two lines, and they were stressed about it, and I was like, I'm running a hotel from my dressing room! [laughs] You have no idea. It seemed like a walk in the park.

MS. HOMES: It keeps things in perspective in a lot of ways.

MR. PAVEL: My biggest problem with so many actors is that they're so self-involved, and this job has definitely prevented me from doing that. And if I ever did have to support myself as an actor down the road, I hope that I would remember everything that I've observed and loathed about people in this industry, and that I will take that to heart and never forget the service people.

MS. HOMES: Do you still feel you have your Midwestern sensibility?

MR. PAVEL: I feel that's what's made me excel at this job. I really relate to my employees. I mean, the Mexican immigrant experience, which is basically all of the hotel staff—that strong Catholic sense of family and work ethic, is very similar to what I grew up with. One of my managers is a guy I brought from Barney Greengrass. We've worked together here for six years. His apartment was on fire, and he called me to see if he could stay at the hotel. I could tell this was a very big deal for him. It was only this moment of total desperation, so he didn't have to sleep in his car. And I was ... Your apartment burned down! Of course you can stay at the hotel! I have empty rooms. And I let him stay here, and the next day I went into the room and he had slept on the couch, because he didn't want to mess the bed and make extra work for the maid.

MS. HOMES: What else do you think is important in describing yourself and the hotel?

MR. PAVEL: What I'm fascinated by is just ... the creative energy. You know, there's something that inherently speaks to me in a lot of people's art and the fact that they're drawn to this place as well. But I always go back to the story that one guest who's been coming here for fourteen years had a psychic come and evaluate the property. She was afraid that there was a ghost and the nine suites kind of freaked her out, so she called in a psychic. The psychic didn't find a ghost, but her consensus was that the Chateau was built on an energy vortex, like Sedona, New Mexico. And she hypothesized that the reason that all sorts of creative people come here to work is that they're feeding off the vortex. I love that story because I opened up the front page of *Rolling Stone* this past month, and it says the Red Hot Chili Peppers just finished their album. And the Chili Peppers were recording their last album in the actual suite. People come here and sit in the lobby and write—my friend wrote her book in the corner there. And part of it's just it's a nice atmosphere and it's quiet, and that you don't get bothered and no one's going to kick you out. Friends always say, Oh, well, now you're general manager of the Chateau, you could go anywhere. But the reality is that I would never want to be general manager anywhere else. I wouldn't be happy anywhere else, because no other hotel would be like this. And it's just funny to me how things evolve in one's life. And that my training in theater and my hobby of acting makes me understand the experience of the guests. In reading the old history, the first manager, Anne Little, was this old character actress who played a squaw in some movies, and I wonder if I'm Anne Little reincarnated!

CHAPTER TEN

Building a Frontier Town

"In the nineteenth century the center of the art world was Paris, in the twentieth century it shifted to New York, and now at the beginning of the twenty-first century there is no dominant center, but everyone agrees L.A. is the hottest city in the art world—the energy is here," says Anne Philbin, director of UCLA's Hammer Museum. Formerly director of New York's Drawing Center, Philbin moved to Los Angeles three years ago. Last summer the Hammer opened an exhibition titled "Snapshot: New Art from Los Angeles" featuring both under-known artists who have been at it for a while and others fresh out of school. "It used to be that when people graduated from art school they moved to New York. Now they're coming to L.A.—it's about real estate. In New York there are no undiscovered, undeveloped areas. L.A. is still a frontier, and it's possible to live and work here and for artists to afford large enough studio spaces to work with a kind of scale and ambition—and artists like good weather too, you know," Philbin says.

In recent years Los Angeles has become a genuine hot spot for both art and architecture—perhaps the most active and interesting in the country. There's been a surge of new galleries, museum expansions, increased attendance at arts-related events, a plethora of first-rate art schools drawing students from around the world. The entertainment and other economies in L.A. are able to support the arts economy.

Architecturally, L.A. has always been a radical outpost. Aesthetically, it is uniquely democratic—the built environment accepting almost anything, which is both the beauty and the horror of it.

Also operative here has been a brand of set design mentality, an aesthetic of transience, impermanence, the knowledge that at any moment a structure could be consumed by geological disaster, which allows for expressive free play in terms of materials and form. For the recent film *My Life as a House,* production designer Dennis Washington had to first construct a neighborhood where there had been none, laying down lawns, walkways, putting up mailboxes, creating facades of houses, and then he had to create a falling-down house for the fictional character, architect George Monroe, to live in. Following that Washington had to design and construct the character's dream house, modeled on a Greene & Greene craftsman-style house and make it in sections so that they could shoot it as the actors were "building" the house in the course of the film. And then ten weeks later when the film was finished they had to demolish everything.

"Architects have always on the one hand been fascinated by the climate and by the very particular geography, the horizontality of the city," says MOCA Director Jeremy Strick. It is a city known for its private spaces, domestic architecture, with an incredible range of modernist and experimental houses designed by Frank Lloyd Wright, Richard Neutra, Rudolph Schindler, John Lautner, Ray and Charles Eames, the Case Study Houses. But the city itself is changing, becoming more public. It is as if Los Angeles has matured, gained confidence, and is transforming the way it thinks about itself. There has been a surge of energy, an urgency to this development. One has a distinct sense that something major is happening here—you can literally watch as the skyline changes. Within blocks of each other in downtown Los Angeles, two world-class buildings are currently under construction—Frank Gehry's Walt Disney Concert Hall and the Cathedral of Our Lady of the Angels by Rafael Moneo. "It's a moment in L.A. that is similar to that time in the construction of great cities, where a few of these projects moving forward could potentially tip the balance between L.A. being continually considered a great place of experimentation but a bit of a backwater and the city becoming one of the great cities," says Los Angeles based architect Michael Maltzen. "It's a city which has lived *off* of its potential for an incredibly long time in terms of its real role in the pantheon of cities, and now it has the potential to transcend, to live *up* to its potential."

A few years ago, while I was interviewing sculptor Richard Serra, the subject of Serra's youth in northern California and its effect on his sense of space and possibility came up.

"I was really born in the sand dunes—there weren't any blacktop streets. So I had to walk through the sand dunes as a kid, and it was kind of like walking through a big, vast, open desert. And the only things that were around were a few eucalyptus trees, right down to the ocean. And I think that hones your eye in a different way. There is something about being from the West that's very, very different. ... If you go back to New York, it's really closer to Europe—and I think that there's something about not being encumbered with a big tradition, if you're from the West, that's healthy. You don't grow up with it all around you. And so, when you finally come to deal with history as it's been served up, you're not paralyzed by it. You just think other people who were around did something interesting, and why not you?" Serra said.

Richard Serra's sense of both the open landscape and the lack of being burdened by history have allowed artists a pioneer's freedom of expression and expansion that is almost without precedent—it is perhaps an uniquely American experience.

Recent examples of that pioneer spirit can be found in L.A.'s Chinatown. Beginning in 1998, a small group of young galleries opened up shop on Chung King Road, part of the ongoing reinvigoration of the downtown area. It wasn't long ago that stores in Chinatown would only be rented to Chinese people with a connection to Chinatown. In the center of the Chung King Road square is a wishing well filled with goldfish, guarded by a statue of Kuan Yin, Chinese goddess of mercy, flip a quarter in and make your deal. These days it's a delightful combination of old and new: shops selling straw hats, bamboo umbrellas, jade, cloisonné, and silk robes alternate with storefront galleries exhibiting the freshest of the fresh. Many of the galleries are run by artists for artists and play host to a variety of events including exhibitions and performances. The cultures mix as they celebrate openings at Hop Louie, a family restaurant that has been there for years—their house fried rice is the best I've ever had. And echoing the general sprawling style of Los Angeles, galleries are scattered all over the city in small clumps, with new ones opening all the time. People here do their gallery hopping by car, spending Saturdays making their way from Chinatown out to Santa Monica to cover it all.

When I started thinking about Los Angeles and the art world, Los Angeles and its culture, I thought of Mark Bennett. Bennett is not only a well-known artist, but he's also a Beverly Hills mailman.

I first got to know Mark Bennett through his artwork—architectural renderings of the homes of television characters. Over a twenty-year period, Bennett sat in front of the television set, sketching, drawing, making blueprint drawings of classic television homes. He hoped that if he could record these houses and their inhabitants, he would become part of their families and they would become part of him.

His is an obsession with domestic life—idealized domestic life as portrayed on television. First exhibited in a bar in Hollywood, the works have been presented in solo shows across the country and have been included in group exhibitions, such as "The Home Show" at the Walker Art Center in Minneapolis and "Made in California: Art, Image and Identity, 1900-2000" at the Los Angeles County Museum of Art.

Mark has rendered the homes of Mike and Carol Brady of *The Brady Bunch,* Rob and Laura Petrie from *The Dick Van Dyke Show,* Lucy and Ricky Ricardo starring in *I Love Lucy,* Oliver and Lisa Douglas, who left New York City for a falling-down house and good country living in *Green Acres,* and the apartments of Mary Richards from *The Mary Tyler Moore Show,* Felix Unger and Oscar Madison from *The Odd Couple* and the Clampetts' Beverly Hills estate as seen on *The Beverly Hillbillies.* He knows exactly where Mary Richards keeps her spare suitcase and where Granny Clampett brews moonshine.

Most recently at Santa Monica's Mark Moore Gallery, Mark exhibited a new project, "As Seen on T.V.," an installation of mama and papa wing and club chairs, puzzles made into a dance patio, curtains, and a Diane Von Furstenberg wrap dress all imprinted with the infamous logo "As Seen on T.V." and alternately "Similar to Those Seen on T.V." The show becomes a wonderful visual play on the implication that being seen on television is tantamount to some sort of cultural stamp of approval, like the Good Housekeeping Seal of Approval.

What becomes clear from looking at Mark Bennett's work is that watching television is not just a collective cultural experience but an instructional one as well—we learn how to live and how others live. Witnessing the ways in which these characters negotiated the space of their faux houses is as much an anthropological investigation as it is a lesson. In these programs we see worlds of possibilities—on television it is possible for fathers and sons to talk about important issues; for mothers and fathers, husbands and wives to argue and recover, for a family to struggle and get on with life. The dysfunction is minimal and is the stuff of situation comedy. On a television show, one can see what a family should be, one can see oneself in the characters, one can see a better life. The focus is ultimately on prosperity, success, and versions of the American Dream.

It was Mark's fantasy to someday build a utopian neighborhood where instead of buying an Italianate villa, a split level, ranch, or a colonial, you'd buy a Rob and Laura, or a Mike and Carol. For Mark, watching television was and is about families.

"It's about finding families. I had a real hard time with mine while I was growing up, so I made these people my families, wanted them to be my families. You don't have to be related. I've got—*Perry Mason:* they're a family to me; they're always up in the middle of the night making coffee, working on briefs for the next day's trial. The *Gilligan's Island* crew—they weren't family but they sure did become one. ... That's the difference between *Star Trek* and *Lost in Space. Lost in Space* really was a family and *Star Trek* was really about employees—there's a difference. ... I'm trying as best I can to live a sitcom life."

Growing up in Chattanooga, Tennessee, Mark's obsession with domestic life started early. On Sunday after church his parents took the family out visiting model houses, dream houses in neighborhoods with fantastic-sounding names. This house-hunting, peeking into the lives of others, was the seed of Mark's interest in observing other families, seeing how people live, what kind of décor they have, how their personalities are expressed, all of it coupled with the desire for a more perfect family, for acceptance.

While a young student teacher working in a rough part of Chattanooga, Bennett's mother encouraged him to take the civil service exam and apply for a position in the post office. A year later, while Bennett was selling shoes in a local mall, he got a letter offering him a job. After six months at the Chattanooga post office, he put in for a transfer—he wanted to go to New York to become an artist. As there were no jobs in New York, he accepted a transfer to Newark, New Jersey, working as a clerk on the midnight shift and after a year transferred to New York's Times Square station, where he worked as a carrier from 1979 to 1985. By then he'd dropped out of art school, written a couple of screenplays, and decided that, "If I'm going to be in this business, I'm going to move to L.A." He sold his apartment, bought a house and, by 1995, the first of his blueprint drawings were hanging in a local bar, the Cobalt Cantina in Silverlake. Here his work was "discovered" by Christopher Ford of the Mark Moore Gallery and things took off for Bennett. Throughout, Mark has kept his job as a postman. He credits the job with giving him an enormous amount of stability, with making his life as an artist possible.

I joined him on his route. "Meet me at eleven on the corner of Roxbury and Wilshire," Mark said. I waited for him on the bench outside the Beverly Hills branch of Neiman Marcus, right next to the employees door, where everyone hangs out, smoking. It's 11:15 a.m.—he's already been at it since 5:30 a.m. Official and adorable with his white pith helmet, shorts, high socks, and the keys to the letter boxes dangling from a brass chain, Mark is a welcome visitor wherever he goes.

It is unexpectedly fascinating—the mood, the tenor, changes from room to room, office to office, door to door. Each is a different world. From the super slick film company with money to burn, to the doctor's office last renovated in the 1950s.

In a town that doesn't see a lot of pedestrian traffic, there is safety to being with the mailman; it provides a screen, maintaining an air of invisibility—otherwise you'd stand out as a suspect. No one except the mailman walks the residential streets of Beverly Hills unnoticed.

All along I'm thinking of questions: What's the most exciting piece of mail you ever delivered? Your worst day as a mailman? How much do you walk in a day? Do you spend your off hours with other postal employees? What about the phrase "going postal"—do you worry about someone going crazy at the post office? What's the deal with dogs and postmen—do you like animals?

We walk up and down the streets at a steady clip with Mark pushing the cart; the only problem taping an interview while walking with the mailman is keeping up and getting him to speak into the microphone.

MR. BENNETT: So what we're doing now, we call the business. Every route has a section of business, a section of apartments, and a section of single family homes. Everybody has a variety of things. Today's a very good day. I'm so glad we've decided to do it today.

MS. HOMES: What makes today a good day?

MR. BENNETT: What happens is: Mondays are heavy because of the weekend. And plus, places are closed on

Saturday. So by the time Tuesday rolls around, it's kind of quiet. Now, by the time Wednesday comes, people are corresponding, they're answering the letters that came out on Monday. So by Wednesday and Thursday, boom!

MS. HOMES: And how does a business's mail differ from residential?

MR. BENNETT: Just volume. I'm what you'd consider the slums of Beverly Hills, believe it or not. This is like not the most prime. Everyone's always been up in the hills, because that's where all the celebrities live. In reality, you never see a celebrity, you just talk to the maid. And no phones, no bathroom, no water. I've always been very lucky. I used to be a substitute on this route. The lady that had this retired, and then I successfully lobbied to get this route. And I've worked all over—which you usually do when you start out. It takes years to get a really good route. Have you noticed your mail delivery in places like New York? Because I worked in New York City, Times Square, for ten years.

MS. HOMES: Yeah, I do notice my mail, because I get a lot of mail.

MR. BENNETT: Do you find the mail to be every day, or just some days?

MS. HOMES: Well, Mondays are very, very heavy. You're right, there is sort of a pattern to it.

MR. BENNETT: They had a forty-two cents due, I don't care. They're sweet to me. And these people, they'll give you a hundred bucks at Christmas. I'm really tight with my people. There's a mailbox in the street and I'll pick that up on the way back. We have to do it on certain times. I have to hit one box at eleven o'clock, I have to hit one box at eleven thirty. I may be off a little bit today.

MS. HOMES: So how long have you had this route?

MR. BENNETT: Five years.

MS. HOMES: And you know a lot of the people on it.

MR. BENNETT: Oh yeah. I go to the Bar Mitzvahs. You get real close to everybody. I don't have a family, so this is kind of good for me. Sometimes you're out, and you're trying to get back, and people are like, can't you stop and say hello? And I'm like, Marge, it's five o'clock and the sun's going down. The barbershop's hilarious. It's been there a hundred years. It was featured prominently in a movie. And Mel Torme had his fatal heart attack in that barbershop.

MS. HOMES: See, Mark, these are the details I need!

MR. BENNETT: Oh, I can tell you some stories that will curl your hair! They have a local ragsheet called *213.* The area code's changed three times. It used to be 213. So it's called *Beverly Hills 213,* and there's another ragsheet called the *Courier.* Well the *213* is all gossip, and it's the most hilarious thing. Here's a doctor who treats only celebs. I love this building because it's sort of scary. I come in the back; they have a secret entrance, and you'll see a famous actress. Every day! Big-time stars—people come and go.

MS. HOMES: What's the 90210 theory?

MR. BENNETT: The 90210 theory is that if you live in 90210 you've arrived. We're actually 90212. So it's still considered pretty much ... Beverly Hills. Morning, Dinah! But not as posh.

MS. HOMES: I love this because you get to open every door in Los Angeles. You're like hi, the mail's here. And they're all different inside!

MR. BENNETT: Yeah, it's one of my favorite buildings, I used to be obsessed with ... I used to tape *The Fugitive* reruns in black-and-white. After work I'd go home and watch *The Fugitive*. I don't watch *Fugitive* any more, but when I come to this building it keeps reminding me of that.

MS. HOMES: Right. Because it is very like that.

MR. BENNETT: It's very like that! Everybody in the building is somehow running scams. I hate that, when they're running scams. Because then you don't know who to call. For example, one of my customers, she was eighty, and she dies. Okay. No relatives, no husband, nothing. ... It's this incredibly spooktacular house. She gives the house to the next of kin, which was like this distant cousin who could care less. So what he's doing is he's living in it with his friends, except he's trying to use her name. It's just awful. So what do you do? I just hate that.

MS. HOMES: Are a lot of people who work in mail, mail people? Do they collect stamps?

MR. BENNETT: Some people are so into it. I got kind of hooked into that philatelic thing. But it didn't last long. They actually have someone who has a separate little counter, where you can go buy stamps. They have sheets that have been canceled and there's all this madness. There's a stamp on an envelope, and they cancel it. They give them away as prizes. I use mine.

MS. HOMES: And what are the big themes for postal workers?

MR. BENNETT: Themes? This is what you live for. Your dream job. Your dream assignment, of which there are several in this town, is when you go in a huge office building. But the dream job is to have what they call a VIL, I don't know what it stands for, but it's an actual post office in an office building. You literally have no supervision. You are your own boss. You make sure that you take care of everything, and everything's done. But other than that. ... These are collection cards. They want to make sure that you collect.

MS. HOMES: That stamps it?

MR. BENNETT: No, you turn in this color today, and tomorrow I'll turn in this color. It's gotten so crazy that they have this little gizmo that you have to deal with all day, that I'll forget to get the mail because I'm worried about this. [laughs]

MS. HOMES: That's amazing. Are they in every box, or just in ... ?

MR. BENNETT: Yes! Every box.

MS. HOMES: Did you get the card for that box, or it's one card for ... ?

MR. BENNETT: No, just one card for both, because you've got to do both. Because the minute you don't … an inspector comes out, it's this big red card that says "do not throw in outgoing mail, bring this back to your supervisor!" And that's how they catch you if you don't collect the mail. Now if you're stupid enough not to collect it, they drop a card on you. I forgot to collect one time on my route, I didn't know it. Or I collected it too early. They dropped a card on me. I come back to the office, and there's your boss standing there like this, tapping her foot. Don't you have something for me? Oh, do you want a sandwich or something? No, no, don't you have something for me? And I'm going no, I don't. Come with me. They took me out in the staff car, and I had to go get it.

MS. HOMES: Is it a tough business?

MR. BENNETT: You're on a time clock. You have one lunch spot every day. And my lunch spot, whether I pack it or buy it, is right here.

MS. HOMES: You mean they tell you where you can sit and have lunch?

MR. BENNETT: Or there's a form you fill out every day that says what time are you having lunch and where will it be.

MS. HOMES: So you can pick where it is but you have to tell them where you're going to be?

MR. BENNETT: I always say Simon's café. Because if something happens, and they need to find me, they can zip over here at 12:30, they know I'm going to be at Simon's café. That's how they do it.

MS. HOMES: And what would they need to find you for?

MR. BENNETT: Believe me, I don't know. Sometimes they have emergencies. Somebody gets sick. Like today.

EPILOGUE

Epilogue

Coming home that night, I find the night watchman standing in the hall, staring at my door—my room key is dangling from the lock.

"Thank God you're here," he says, "I wasn't quite sure what had happened."

I assume that when I went out I simply forgot to take the key with me.

"Do you want me to go in with you and make sure everything is okay?" he asks.

"Okay, sure," I say, although I am not the least bit afraid. Together we open the door to make sure that no one has taken the key in the door as an invitation to enter. All is calm, quiet.

"Looks good," I say to the man, "thank you."

"You're that super-cool writer girl," he says to me.

Validation.

"Thank you again," I say. "And good night."

The night before I leave Los Angeles, I call downstairs and ask the clerk at the front desk to buzz me if Romulo, the overnight waiter, begins to sing. For years I've been hearing about Romulo's impromptu late-night performances but had never managed to stay up late enough to see one.

At 2:30 in the morning the phone rings, yanking me from a dream.

"I hope I didn't wake you," the fellow at the desk says. "I figured you'd be up late, writing."

I assure him that despite the fact that I was sound asleep, it's fine.

"Romulo's singing," he says.

"I'll be right down."

Romulo Laki is the night waiter, working the 10:30 P.M.– 6:30 A.M. shift. He's been at the Chateau for fifteen years. Usually I see him only in passing, he comes on as I'm going off to dinner and then off to bed. They say he's the one with all the stories, he's the one who's up all night, who sees everything, who knows exactly what's going on where—after all, he delivers the snacks. And when it gets late, and things are slow, he brings out his guitar and begins to sing. I find him in the lobby, surrounded by a group of slightly drunk young people. He's singing John Denver's "Country Road," followed by the Rolling Stones' "As Tears Go By," a song Mick Jagger wrote long ago for Marianne Faithfull—which I find extremely poignant since I've seen her here at the hotel on occasion. There is about Romulo a kind of steadiness—there's also much talk about his black hair, whether it's really his or in some way sprayed on to fill in what's disappeared with age. He segues into a nice Elvis medley and then asks if I'd like to hear a song he's written himself, a Spanish love song. It is as if he's singing the guests to sleep, offering them a lullaby which they take as a cue to wind down, to call it a night; they sign their checks and stumble off to bed.

....

My time in Los Angeles is over. And while I've come to know the city in a purely navigational and geographic sense, I still don't have a clue as to the truth or the heart of Los Angeles. I can drive the city from end to end. I know the order of the boulevards descending down from Sunset. I know where to get on and off the freeways, but I can't begin to say that I know Los Angeles. What becomes apparent is that there is no one center, in all the sprawl there are thousands of wholly complete worlds, unique, disparate, enormously diverse. It reminds me of Washington, D.C., in that the divides between race and class are extreme. One can easily exist in a Los Angeles that is entirely white, or black, or hispanic, and unless one makes an effort to bridge the gap between cultures, the gap will continue to grow. It is dangerously easy to pretend that there is no world outside one's own. In this city, it is every man for himself; each person makes his own reality. There are very few collective experiences—the weather, the traffic, the Earth itself.

And although I still may not know Los Angeles well, I have come to know the Chateau Marmont intimately. Around the world there are great hotels, legendary hotels, grand hotels, hotels known for their architecture, for their service, for the history of who has stayed there before. There are rarified boutique hotels, luxury getaways, hotels in places where man has barely trod, hotels where there used to be hotels. And then there is the Chateau Marmont.

It is a place where not just anything goes, but everything goes. There is always someone being photographed for a magazine in the lobby, a fashion shoot by the pool, or even in the pool. There are readings, wine tastings, musical performances, casting directors holding auditions in their suites. Writers who aren't even staying here bring their computers to the lobby and sit down to work and absolutely everyone has their meetings here. As Billy Wilder famously once said about the Chateau, "I'd rather sleep in a bathroom than in another hotel."

Acknowledgments

I would like to thank the following for sharing with me their knowledge and impressions of Los Angeles: Mark Bennett, Tom Henyey, Dr. Fred Kogen, Tommy and Bobbi Farrell, Virginia McDowall, Hal Riddle, Griffin Dunne, Jennifer Beals, John Waters, Eve Babitz, Lisa Phillips, Todd Eberle, Ellen Krass, Anne Philbin, M. G. Lord, Jeremy Strick, Michael Maltzan, Richard Serra, Marc H. Glick, Marie V. Sanford, Dan Sonenberg, Amy Gross, and the Staff at The Motion Picture and Retirement Fund, Wintec Energy, and La Quinta Resort and Club. I would also like to thank Peter Gay and Pamela Leo and the Center for Scholars and Writers at The New York Public Library. My agents, Andrew Wylie, Sarah Chalfant and Jin Auh. Larry Porges and Elizabeth Newhouse at National Geographic. And at the Chateau Marmont, great thanks to Andre Balazs, Philip Pavel, Pat Abedi, Carol O'Brien, Erin Foti, Romulo Laki, and the hotel staff.

ABOUT THE AUTHOR

A. M. Homes is the author of the novels *Jack, In a Country of Mothers, The End of Alice,* and *Music for Torching;* the short story collections *The Safety of Objects* and *Things You Should Know;* and the artists' book *Appendix A:.* Her fiction and nonfiction appear frequently in magazines such as: *Art Forum, Granta, Harper's, McSweeney's, The New Yorker, The New York Times Magazine,* and *Vanity Fair.* She is the recipient of numerous awards including Guggenheim and National Endowment for the Arts fellowships. She lives in New York City.

This book is set in Garamond 3, designed by
Morris Fuller Benton and Thomas Maitland
Cleland in the 1930s, and Monotype Grotesque,
both released digitally by Adobe.

Printed by R. R. Donnelley and Sons on
Gladfelter 60-pound Thor Offset smooth
white antique paper.

Dust jacket printed by Miken Companies.
Color separation by Quad Graphics.

Three-piece case of Ecological Fiber orange side
panels with Sierra black book cloth as the spine
fabric. Stamped in Lustrofoil metallic silver.